# GET YOUR DREAM JOB

Ebere Ujam-Ojadua

authorHOUSE®

AuthorHouse™
1663 Liberty Drive
Bloomington, IN 47403
www.authorhouse.com
Phone: 1 (800) 839-8640

Published by AuthorHouse  03/02/2017

ISBN: 978-1-5246-7240-9 (sc)
ISBN: 978-1-5246-7239-3 (e)

Print information available on the last page.

*"Going for an interview can be a huge task when you are not prepared, knowing what to say to convince your interviewer is very important. When you prepare adequately, your chances of getting the job above your peers will be better. To prepare you for success in your interview, this book has been designed just for that."*

*Ebere Ujam-Ojadua*

# Acknowledgments

This book would not have been possible without the support and encouragement I received along the way to realize my vision. Special thanks to God almighty for giving me life, and for the grace to complete this book. My deepest gratitude goes to my parents, for insisting that I had a good education, and to my mother for her unfaltering love and belief in me. My parents worked long and hard to give me the foundation that enabled me pursue my dreams and I am very indebted to them.

Special thanks to my brother; Hon Dr. Chukwuemeka Ujam and his family for their never ending support and belief in me, I am forever grateful. Of course to the rest of my family I say a very big thank you for your love and support too.

I would also like to thank Nicole for her editorial contribution towards this great book; to all my mentors for their motivations and support.

To all my friends, colleagues and well-wishers who helped me through the process of making my dream a reality, I owe each and every one of you a huge debt of gratitude.

*Ebere Ujam-Ojadua*

# FOREWORD

Every other day, numerous job seekers reach out to recruitment agencies, online-job portals, career coaches and job centers to help them find a job, yet they find very little that they are suited to. For the majority of job seekers, they lack the required knowledge and skill-sets needed to earn these jobs.

**Get Your Dream Job** was written with all of these in view – To give you a polished CV/Resume and outstanding interview performance. This book will save you a lot of time and money consulting a career coach.

There is undoubtedly a gap in the market for this book and its arrival couldn't be timelier; the global economy has turned people from all backgrounds and qualifications into job seekers. This book deals with the paramount challenges people face as job hunters. **Get Your Dream Job** will walk you through right from the best way to write and structure your CV/Resume, to preparing for interview and hitting the jackpot on the big day.

Getting your initial application right will set the foundation for every other stage of success up the ladder. Providing advice and support all the way through, **Get Your Dream Job** is a companion guide from beginning to the end of the job search process.

**Get Your Dream Job** offers several unique features that other books within the career coaching book market do not provide. Other books tend to focus on one aspect only of the job search process – you might have to buy a book about writing a winning CV/Resume and another about interview preparation techniques. This book has been deliberately written in an easy-going style; the hard work is all in the job search, so by contrast, the book should be an easy read. There are case studies and special focus sections that give real life examples into different aspects of the job search process, so even if the particulars of each scenario don't resonate with you, the background of their story will.

I believe that every human being has great potential to succeed. It is no secret that as human beings go, we are way happier when we work in the right job. It becomes more of passion and less work. I hope that this book will show you how to grab your desired job without struggle.

Best of luck.

**Daniel Ojadua**
*Author, Team Motivator & Business Strategist.*

# ENDORSEMENTS

The title says it all. The Author has elucidated in simple terms what it takes to get a job!! I am especially proud of my kid sister, as she has always had a knack for the literary arts. The effort is commendable. This is a must read and I know before putting it to print quite a number of people around the author have used these techniques successfully.

Ebere has always been exceptional in all that she does, it's of no surprise to me that she could come up with such an excellent write up, this is one of the easiest and straight to the point books I have ever read.

I definitely recommend this book not just to job seekers but also entrepreneurs as guide to finding the right person to hire. I am endorsing this book on behalf of the entire family. We believe in you kid sister. The sky is your starting point. God bless.

*Chukwuemeka Ujam, PhD*

If preparing for a job interview has always baffled you, this book is the key to unlock its mysteries. In my years of training people I've never run across a book that made 'Interview' success so easy and interesting. The language is simple and easy to read. I must also commend the efforts of the writer in making this available at this crucial time. I therefore recommend this book to every value adding individual.

This is your day!!!!

*Dele Osunmakinde*
***CEO ENTERPRISING NIGERIA***

"Get Your Dream Job" is an incredible masterpiece that is a 'MUST HAVE' for every new and seasoned job seeker.

Written in an easy to read and fun style, it communicates the practical 'how to's' in getting your dream job.

It answers questions from both the Human Resource perspective as well as the 'what to do' from the job seeker's point of view.

It's fantastic!

Please read it before you ask me for a job!

***SteveHARRIS Life Strategist & Managing Consultant, EdgeEcution***

# Contents

Introduction ............................................................... xvii

  What is a CV/Resume? ......................................... xvii

  How long should my CV/Resume be? ................... xviii

  Who is this book for? ............................................. xix

  Consistency is key .................................................. xx

  Defining your USP (Unique Selling Proposition) ...... xx

  The purpose of the interview ................................. xxi

Chapter 1:  Planning Your CV/Resume ......................... 1

  Why is a CV/Resume so important today? ............... 1

  Why is it so important to get the CV/Resume right? ...... 2

  What puts your CV/Resume ahead of the game against a
  competitor with equal attributes? ........................... 2

  Decisions to make before you start writing your CV/Resume ...... 3

  What kind of paper should I print my CV/Resume on? ...... 4

  What type of font should I use? .............................. 5

  A note on font size ................................................. 6

  What to say and how to say it ................................. 7

Chapter 2:  Writing your CV/Resume ........................... 8

  CV/Resume templates for different sectors ............ 10

  Skills CV/Resume Template ................................... 14

  Classic CV/Resume Template ................................. 19

  The cover letter ..................................................... 19

  So now you are all ready to go! ............................. 21

  When to get creative with your CV/Resume and when to
  keep it plain? ........................................................ 22

Should I include a thumbnail photo of myself?....................23

Getting the tone right .................................................24

Gaps in my career history............................................24

Let's recap: tips on presenting your CV/Resume......................29

Breaking it down and making sense. ..................................31

How to articulate your attributes...................................34

Interests and achievements ..........................................35

Targeting your CV/Resume.............................................39

Disabilities – should I disclose in a CV/Resume?....................40

Reasons why you might find it useful to disclose your
disability............................................................43

Chapter 3:  Interviews – Preparation and Performance.............. 46

Researching the Company..............................................48

Types of interview .................................................50

Managing closed questions...........................................65

Arriving for the interview .........................................66

First impressions...................................................67

A little research into the X factor that clinches the job..........71

The Panic Factor: how to overcome interview fears .................72

Chapter 4:   The Most Common Interview Categories of Questions ...77

Recognizing what interviewers are looking for.......................77

How to make sure you put the 3C essentials across: a
word on articulation................................................79

How many interviewers will there be? ...............................82

Communication Skills................................................83

Body language.......................................................87

Negotiation and persuasion .........................................90

Example of 'Emotional' Persuasion or Negotiation. ..................90

Explaining your strengths and weaknesses: more helpful
acronyms............................................................96

More typical interview questions................................... 103

Chapter 5:   Tailoring the Interview ............................. 110

About the company................................................. 110

Why do you want to work for our company?...........................111
Why are you applying for this job? ......................................111
How do you deal with problems?...........................................112
Describe a situation where you had to deal with a difficult
person. ...................................................................................114
Why did you leave your last job? ..........................................115
Where do you see yourself in life in five years? ....................124
So what can you offer that no one else can?.........................125

Conclusion: Cardinal Rules, Cardinal Sins And How Not to
        Do An Interview.......................................................131
Ten Cardinal Sins of Interviewing........................................133
Failing the stuck in the lift test............................................137
Interviews: how not to do it ...............................................138

# INTRODUCTION

# WHAT IS A CV/RESUME?

A Curriculum Vitae (CV/Resume) is an outline of a person's educational and professional history that most job applications require before shortlisting candidates for interview. The term 'CV/Resume' is used in the United Kingdom while the term 'Resume' tends to be used in the United States and other non-European countries.

Having a well-written, up to date CV/Resume is the most flexible and convenient way to apply for jobs. You have complete control over making sure that it conveys your personal details in such a way that they present you in the best possible light. A CV/Resume is a marketing document for selling yourself. Why? Because a recruiter invests in you financially and professionally, you need to "sell" your skills, abilities, qualifications and experience, to employers, to convince them that you are the one to invest in. Your CV/Resume needs to make you stand out as an individual that the company can't do without, once they have read your CV/Resume and then interviewed you. Once you get the basics right when you compile it, you can use it to make several applications to different employers in a specific career area. The most important thing to keep in mind is that while your CV/Resume is the basis for getting you that interview, it is far from a 'one size fits all' document. This book will show you how to write a CV/Resume that gives you the best chance of getting that job, and how to tailor your CV/Resume to each individual application. So what are some of the specifics that this book will walk you through?

Here are some examples that we will look at in more detail:

- How much contact information to provide and where to place it on your CV/Resume.
- Stating all of your professional qualifications on the front page, because these are an essential part of the recruiter's criteria for selection.
- Ensuring that your qualifications are displayed clearly.
- Including all related qualifications and additional training courses, as well as professional accreditations, additional academic study, and so on.
- Showcasing your 'extra' attributes and experience by making your volunteering experience, hobbies and interests relevant to the job you are applying for.

We will also walk through the 'what not to do' minefields of CV/Resume writing. For example, you don't mention reasons for leaving your previous job on your CV/Resume. This is about your strengths and positives, not about your personal/professional struggles, (though be prepared to be asked about these at interview). Also, details about current salary of what you expect from the job you are applying for are better suited to the covering letter or discussed during the interview session.

## HOW LONG SHOULD MY CV/RESUME BE?

The jury is out on this one. Many career coaches suggest that two pages or maximum of three if absolutely necessary is as much as recruiters will read. Remember, interview candidates are selected from a 15 second glance through a CV/Resume so the most important information needs to be clear, concise and strategically placed where you want the recruiter to read it. Some recruiters will accept a longer CV/Resume from applicants who have held senior positions for a number of years. As a rule of thumb, any professional experience that stretches back beyond 10 years needs to be listed concisely in one or two lines that showcase the importance of this experience.

If you are applying for a senior level job it is assumed that you know certain HR basics for example, such as employment law and disciplinary procedures, so there is no need to go into too much detail. You will be expected to show your most up to date knowledge in detail. Remember too that in order to distinguish between two good candidates, most employers will look out for which one has gone the extra mile, taking on extra responsibilities and gaining lateral experience that they can bring to the job. So before writing your CV/Resume you will be thinking about how many people you have managed, who you reported to and what role you have played on a managerial or operational board.

Do you have experience of managing projects? Of adapting your professional experience successfully to jobs in other sectors? The wider your range of experience, the more versatile your skill set becomes, and this is exactly what employers are looking for. A good manager's favourite word should be 'delegate' – you want your line manager to trust that you can get on with your job without hourly supervision, and that you can problem solve and improvise if things get a bit sticky now and again (as happens in any job).

## WHO IS THIS BOOK FOR?

Anyone who is applying for a job! Senior executives who need to refresh on their CV/Resume writing and interview technique as much as graduates fresh out of the University. Whether you have high end professional experience or you are still forming your character on everyday experience, everything that contributes to your strengths (yes, even your mistakes) is relevant to a job application.

- What makes you tick?
- What is that particular thing that you most enjoy doing?
- What projects did you embark on while in \University?
- What extra-curricular activities where you involved in?

If you are able to answer one or two of the above questions, it shows that you possess two or more employable skills.

Subjects like project management, extra-curricular work and leisure, and the question of 'what makes you tick?' apply equally to senior applicants. An employer wants to see that you lead a personal life outside of work, and that you are motivated to make your time off interesting and varied.

## CONSISTENCY IS KEY

It is very important to keep your CV/Resume consistent. Sure, you will tailor it to each individual job but you need to sing the most important facts about yourself to the same tune. What you write on your CV/Resume and how you format it has to sell you clearly and spectacularly. A recruiter will pick up on any inaccuracies, and the most dazzling content on the page will be lost if the format is too messy, too crowded or too zany. Highlight your most relevant work experience and give the least number of lines to the least relevant. List your jobs and qualifications in reverse chronological order. Provide details of who you have worked for: the company name, the sector they operate in, their address, your job title and your responsibilities. Our templates will show you how to do this – once you have found a format that you like, stick to it consistently throughout. Make it your own CV/Resume writing style and if it works, use it again and again! It is important to show solid career progression, and to showcase it.

## DEFINING YOUR USP (UNIQUE SELLING PROPOSITION)

In order to showcase yourself as the most suitable applicant for the job you need to clearly highlight the value you will add to your potential employer. The goal is to set yourself apart from other professionals. Don't generalize, state your areas of expertise and highlight the experience that supports your expertise. List all relevant skills such as language skills (especially for multinationals) and additional IT skills. Don't forget to highlight your excellent communication skills – your employer wants to be reassured that they are hiring someone who can be trusted to represent the company well. That's the basis, then it's time to showcase you as a whole so that you have the edge on an equally qualified candidate. You need to think about how to make the recruiter genuinely interested in you as a person and as a potential addition to the company. Make sure that you can explain all gaps in your employment history; these tend to set off alarm bells for recruiters if they don't seem to have been filled with understandable reasons. It is one definite area that interviewers will try to probe. Also, as I explained earlier -- you may not include reasons on your CV/Resume for leaving a job but you may be asked about this during interviews, so have your answers prepared. (If you've been hit by a bolt of anxiety, fear not, we cover 'Reasons for Leaving' in Chapter 5).

## THE PURPOSE OF THE INTERVIEW

So with a winning CV/Resume, what is the big deal about the interview? Firstly, it is for the interviewer to see if you match the requirements of the job. These will naturally vary with different jobs but all interviews want to get a sense of:

- Your personal qualities
- How articulately you express yourself
- How natural and professional you can be under pressure
- Your motivation and enthusiasm

The recruiters will already have an indication of these from your initial application but now the interview is their opportunity to assess you in person. Some great CV/Resumes turn out some disastrous candidates, and some wonderful interviewees were shortlisted purely by chance, having submitted poor CV/Resumes.

It's natural to feel that the interview is an opportunity for the recruiter to scrutinize you. In a sense, it is – let's not mince our words here and pretend that it is something else. But rather than allowing this to destroy your chances because of paralyzing anxiety, look on it also a) as your chance to sell yourself, and b) as your chance to scrutinize the company. You get to meet some of the key people who work with the organization you have applied to: source them out, size them up, and assess them. Are they offering what you want? Do they have the values of a company you would want to work for? Keep in mind that an interview is a two-way process, and this will help you to remain calm. You might feel, having spent 30 minutes in a room with the interview panel that this company is not right for you. Be selective, you don't have to fling yourself at the first job you are offered.

In the second half of this book! We'll walk you through what kind of questions to prepare for. There are no right or wrong answers to interview questions as long as you keep the tone appropriate for the situation. Indulge yourself in outlandish replies and you probably won't get your foot any further through the company door. How you come across is as important as what you say. Be yourself – if you have to put on a completely false act to get through the interview, is this really the right job for you? They will see through it and you will feel unhappy at having sold yourself out. If you cannot be yourself in an interview and put across what you are good at, passionate about, etc. the company doesn't deserve you.

That's the bottom line.

We'll also look at any factors that you feel might put you at a disadvantage for the job. If you have a potential difficulty (e.g. poor exam results or a disability), should you disclose this at the start or the end of the interview? In your CV/Resume or cover letter even? According to research by Jones and Gordon of Duke University, candidates appeared more likeable if weaknesses were disclosed early in the interview and strengths towards the end. Sure, it's hard to have confidence in how you come across if you explain your weaknesses first and your strengths later. Just bear this in mind: you are entitled to be interviewed in full, so you will have the opportunity to put both aspects across. The key is to come in confidently and make a good impression (we will look at this later), then explain your weaknesses when a relevant time comes up, and then bring the final third of the interview to a strong close by explaining your strengths, how they reinforce your skills and how they overcome your weaknesses. The panel will be impressed by someone who is willing to be honest and open about their weaknesses (there is not one person on the planet who doesn't have some kind of weakness). They will be more impressed with your explanation of how you use your problem-solving ability, your initiative and your strengths to overcome your weaknesses. That's the sign of a really valuable employee. Jones and Gordon explain from their research that candidates who disclosed potential problems early on were thought by interviewers to have more integrity and strength of character, and thus were not attempting to mislead them. Candidates who mentioned strengths (such as having been awarded a scholarship) later in the interview appeared more modest than those who blurted it out at the first opportunity, thus seeming boastful. So with all this in mind I hope that these topics have already sparked off some new ideas for you, and helped you to feel more confident about going for that job!

# Chapter 1

# PLANNING YOUR CV/RESUME

## WHY IS A CV/RESUME SO IMPORTANT TODAY?

There are a few reasons for this. Social media networking is one of them – it is easy for anyone to put a profile on LinkedIn that has no accurate information about them. Recruiters do look at Facebook, Twitter, LinkedIn, etc. to get a sense of their potential candidates, but how do they know that what they are reading is true?

Recruitment in the digital era can be a little like online dating. A company can advertise a job as being the best career the lucky candidate could be offered, having them move hundreds of miles to take up the job offer, to find that the company has no scruples or integrity. They control all of their employees so no-one ever gets to do what the job spec promised. Or, a company can think they've found the ideal candidate only to find that they don't hold all the necessary qualifications, or they've claimed to be fit enough for a job that involves physical work only to find that the last time they worked anywhere was two years ago as a cleaner.

*These examples are the 'baddies' of online dating* – the photograph is five years out of date, or someone promises to be respectful and caring but turns out to be a bully and a control freak. Unfortunately, it's harder to get to the bottom of what a company is really like. They have the advantage over you of being able to check you out just by reading your CV/Resume and then checking out its veracity by contacting any of the companies listed, or your referees. So your CV/Resume is where you need to be truthful and to make yourself dazzle off the page. In a certain sense of the word, you are applying blindly to the company – you won't really find out what they are like until you get your foot in the door, even if it is just for an interview. Your CV/Resume, on the other hand, is the company's first true picture of who you are.

## WHY IS IT SO IMPORTANT TO GET THE CV/RESUME RIGHT?

If job recruitment is a bit like online dating, your CV/Resume is your chance to speed-date your potential employer. The average length of time that s/he spends reading your CV/Resume is 15 seconds. So you need to look your best, know how to present yourself in the best way, in the most concise way, and as the employer's best 'match.' In those 15 seconds the recruiter is consciously looking for certain key pieces of information about you while unconsciously, less obvious pieces of information are also making an impression on them.

## WHAT PUTS YOUR CV/RESUME AHEAD OF THE GAME AGAINST A COMPETITOR WITH EQUAL ATTRIBUTES?

This can often be a tough call, and it's where you need to think really creatively about what makes you unique. Why do your friends think you're awesome? Why did your colleagues genuinely miss about you after you left every previous employment or work experience? When you're neck and neck with another candidate, the deciding factor is often about taking your CV/Resume by the scruff of the neck and giving it an extra push. Have you volunteered on a cancer care ward or any charity organization? Have you raised lots of money for your local community, or set up a local volunteer project for an aspect of community development such as buildings and green spaces, care of the elderly, care of children etc. Ever written an outstanding piece of investigative journalism or produced a science paper that has been applauded by your university professor as being exciting and original?

What is the most unusual thing about you (that is appropriate to bring up at an interview)? Having webbed feet doesn't count! It goes back again to your Unique Selling Proposition – what makes you unique? What about you inspire others? Don't limit yourself to the heroics of an original science paper. If you have taken time off work to look after a terminally ill family member, you've got a depth and resilience to your personality that most people could only dream of. (Hint: you probably won't know the answer to these questions yourself – it's time to meet up with friends and family members for coffees and see what answers they give).

## DECISIONS TO MAKE BEFORE YOU START WRITING YOUR CV/RESUME

### What's the deadline?

Do I have time to submit my CV/Resume and cover letter for the job I'm applying for? Here's an example of what can go wrong:

> Christine had nearly 10 years of working in the mental health sector, and had worked her way up to senior positions through commitment and hard work. First she was made a team leader, and eventually she managed an entire stand-alone crisis mental health unit. A job came up that she was really interested in: managing director of a well-known UK mental health charity. The problem was that she saw the job advert the same day that her application was due in.
>
> She updated her CV/Resume and wrote a comprehensive cover letter in a hurry, and on rereading these the content was fine. She was confident that she was in with a good chance. She printed them off as she got ready to go straight to the headquarters and deliver them by hand. She plucked the pages out of the printer

to find nothing but black smudges, and time was pressing on. Not good at all. She hadn't time to run out for black ink, but what she did have in her colour cartridge was plenty of navy ink – should she? Shouldn't she? She decided that this was her only option, not having enough time on her side to do anything else. So she printed her CV/Resume and cover letter in navy ink, slipped them into a brown A4 envelope and ran out the front door … in a storm of rain and wind … to her car.

She found the address of the headquarters with no problem, but there was no parking anywhere nearby. The upshot is that she ran through the wind and the rain, the swirling autumn leaves, and burst into the headquarters reception, glasses steamed up and crooked on her face, hair dripping wet, and looking as wild as the weather outside. So much for her calm and collected 'self-delivery' – the envelope was sopping, she hadn't used black ink, and she had just a tad of hysteria in her voice when she implored of the receptionist: 'you're sure you'll bring it up to HR … you're sure you'll bring it up to HR?'!

The moral of the story? Be prepared and on time when you write your CV/Resume and cover letter. Make sure you have enough black ink and enough time to post it to the recruiter, or if you're going to hand deliver it get a taxi to bring you right to the company's front door! Your CV/Resume presents to the employer a 'pre-interview' you. I'm sure that receptionist told HR that a mad woman had just barged into their office and thrust a soggy, navy CV/Resume at him.

## WHAT KIND OF PAPER SHOULD I PRINT MY CV/RESUME ON?

Think carefully too about how your CV/Resume will look and feel. What kind of paper are you going to choose? Don't go for anything too glossy – the ink can smudge easily on it before it reaches the recruiter's desk, and too glossy can sometimes be difficult to read. Matt paper provides a better surface for reading text. How much information you need to put on your CV/Resume will decide the size of font you use. If you haven't had much work experience you can use a slightly larger font but not outlandishly large. It is fine to have a one page CV/Resume if that's all it takes to lay out your qualifications and experience. If you have a lot of work experience you need to think about how to phrase it succinctly. Do not try to squeeze it all in with tiny font, you'll give your recruiter a headache and will be forever associated with their eye strain. Also check with HR about what format they want the CV/Resume presented in – if they want a hard copy make sure to print off several copies for yourself. If they want to receive your application electronically, check whether they want you to send yours as word doc. or pdf, and make sure to allow yourself enough time to convert from one format to another. Often we think we have IT technology all figured out until we have to spend six hours fighting with word to pdf conversion!

## WHAT TYPE OF FONT SHOULD I USE?

'Times New Roman' and 'Courier' are a hangover from the old typewriter days, and when computer word processing first took over from the typewriter. It's the standard font for most pulp fiction publications, though digital printing technology now makes it much easier for book format designers to integrate different types of font with images (think of medical textbooks for example).

Many CV/Resumes are read on-screen now, as email applications are becoming more popular with recruiters. This has put poor old 'Times New Roman' somewhat in the dark ages of typescript (indeed, it was first used on Trajan's column, 2,000 years ago!), and brought 'Arial', 'Verdana' and 'Calibri' as being screen-friendly alternatives (that are also much easier for people with dyslexia or visual impairment to read). It all comes down to the difference between serifs or sans font. 'Times New Roman' is the standard windows 'Serif' font and 'Arial' is the standard windows 'sans' font. So what's the difference between them? Sans fonts don't have the curly bits on letters. As you can see they're cleaner and more modern than Times or Georgia and they also look larger in the same "point" size (the point size simply being how big the letters are on the page.) 'Serifs' fonts have a more contemporary appearance to them; not overly decorated, and their attractiveness is emphasised by the clean lines. Arial and Times New Roman have become so common that they can be a little boring to the eye. The more contemporary alternatives are 'Calibri', 'Lucida Sans' or 'Verdana'. Trust me, when an interviewer has scores of applications to get through, even the direst content will have a chance of being read, simply because it looks neat, presentable and attractive on the page.

## A NOTE ON FONT SIZE

Font size is normally 12 points for the normal font with larger sizes for sub-headings and headings. My personal favourite CV/Resume body text font is 10 point 'Verdana' or 'Lucida Sans' with 12 or 14 points for sub headings. A 14 points font size is too big for the normal body font on a CV/Resume – it wastes space and can look crude. Worse, it can seem as if you're trying to cover up lack of experience by filling out space on your CV/Resume with large lettering. On the other hand, eight or nine points are far too small to be easily readable by everyone, especially in 'Times New Roman', which should not be used in sizes less than 11 points.

Although many people use 12 points, some research on this suggested that a slightly smaller point size CV/Resumes (within reason) were perceived as being more intellectual! So it's all a case of using your own intellect to find a balance, keeping this advice in mind. So your rule of thumb is that 14 is definitely too large, and 11 is the minimum acceptable size.

# WHAT TO SAY AND HOW TO SAY IT

So it's one thing knowing how to write up the CV/Resume in terms of appearance, layout, spacing, and so on. But now that I am ready to write it up, I can't think of a damn word to put down on this piece of paper that will be so influential in my short and long-term future. And when I do think of what to say, can I be natural or do I have to word everything more formally? The answer is somewhere in between. Being natural can mean anything from bantering with your friends to putting yourself across in a professional situation without sounding too stiff and rehearsed.

The answer is to try to come across as being professional and articulate. If you are confident enough in how you speak you will be able to strike a balance between having a nice turn of phrase but also of using appropriate language. Research has also found that unnecessary use of complex words or hard to read fonts give a bad impression; people who use simple, clear language are rated as more intelligent. Why? Because they are confident enough in their skills and qualifications to state them clearly rather than attempting to dress them up in verbose language that not even a chief executive could be expected to understand.

At the other end of the scale of perfection, The Recruitment and Employment Commission says that about half of all CV/Resumes received by recruitment consultants contain spelling or grammatical errors. Candidates aged between 21 and 25 are most likely to make these mistakes and graduates in this age group are twice as likely to make mistakes as those who did not go on to university. For younger generations, be careful too to watch how 'text-speak' has made its way into your everyday use of the English language. This may sound pedantic, but you would be surprised how many applicants forget to spell out words in their full form, or refer to themselves as 'i' instead of 'I'.

So with all of those naughty spelling habits weeded out, the next chapter is going to walk you through exactly how to start writing up your application using phrasing that feels comfortable to you, conveys what you need to the employer, and makes for good reading! If an employer finds your CV/Resume compelling, she is going to want to invite you to an interview to see if you are as compelling in real life

# CHAPTER 2

# WRITING YOUR CV/RESUME

Now that you are ready to put your fingers to the keyboard, this is your chance to create and present the best, most unique product that a company could want – you!! In the current economic climate, companies regard themselves as investing in 'assets' rather than people. They want your input to be instrumental in keeping its profit margin healthy and contributing to good spirit amongst the staff team. Though you are, in the best possible way, demonstrate why you should be bought into for the job over someone else. Although there's no 'one-sizefits-all' solution to writing a CV/Resume, there are some simple guidelines that everyone, whether they have two years or 25 years of work experience, would do well to follow. The advice I give you in these guidelines will dramatically improve your chances of standing out, securing an interview and eventually getting the job.

The first thing to do when crafting your CV/Resume is to focus on your competencies. Never lose sight of what potential employers are looking for. If you buy a new house, you listen to the estate agent's explanation of it and then view it, looking for outstanding features that make you certain that it's the one you want to purchase. If you can show through your CV/Resume that you meet their operational (a boring word that encapsulates the daily work that keeps a company running) requirements and can provide your dazzling professional competency, then you can be sure of getting interviewed. Obviously, getting into the interviewee's chair is your ultimate opportunity to engage them with your magnetic personality, but to get yourself there you have *got* to capture the very best of you and your experience in writing, on your CV. So carefully study the job description and person specification, and tailor your CV/Resume to match these essential attributes.

If you look on writing your CV/Resume as being your sales pitch to the employer, then your personal profile is your opener. It has to grab them and compel them. This should come below your professional profile with a message strong enough to make you stand out from the crowd. *Do* avoid putting down any generic skills because the employer will have read them so many times she will be blind to them. Hundreds and hundreds of people apply for the same job nowadays, so your CV/Resume has to stand out from plenty of other suitable applicants. Your professional profile focuses more on your professional qualifications and your professional development through experience in specific sectors and areas of expertise, such as project management or experience garnered while managing large teams.

Here is an example of how one graduate did this on their CV/Resume: *"All of my work experiences have involved working within a team-based culture. This grounded me in the experience of planning, organisation, coordination and commitment."* Good stuff so far; what they are essentially saying is that they are an excellent team-player, good at coordinating their planned workload in conjunction with what their colleagues are doing, so that when the work gets done, it's useful in the bigger context of the entire project. *Doing these as a team rather than an individual requires a dedicated approach and respect for my colleagues. The daily outcome of this was that, in retail for example, this ensured that daily sales targets were met, tasks were distributed evenly amongst all staff, and effective communication was promoted throughout the team."* This person's CV/Resume will stand out a mile for the wrong reasons if they are after a loneworker position. But it will shine if good teamwork skills are one of the main requirements of the job.

# CV/RESUME TEMPLATES FOR DIFFERENT SECTORS

Certain industries and establishments have a recommended format in order to capture the most important and relevant information about you. If you are applying for an academic job for example, they don't really want to know in detail about your past 10 years work experience (unless it is related to academia). What they *do* want to know about is how far you have taken your studies – Masters? Ph.D.? And in addition to this, someone applying for an academic career is expected to have published lots of research papers and presented these verbally at academic conferences.

Let's have a look at some different types of CV/Resume templates for different sectors. ***On the next page is a standard CV/Resume layout:***

**Name**

**Address (not your full address – that can be supplied later)**

**Phone: Mobile:**

**Email:**

**Professional Profile**

In a few sentences summarize your career achievements to date and where you want to go from here.

**Work Experience:**

A list of all jobs you have held, most recent first then working back in reverse chronological order.

Include company/institution name, job title, duties/tasks and dates.

**Responsibilities:**

* List here the requirements of your job role in your most recent positions.

### Educational Background

Undergraduate and postgraduate degrees, including institution, title of degree, dates and grade achieved.

### Additional qualifications, training and accreditations

Achievements:
* Related to your responsibilities, what improvements did you bring to your workplace? (Also list previous achievements that put you ahead of the game for this job). And don't forget to include your life achievements – these are really important too because they show something about your personality.

**Hobbies and interests:** Swimming, watching TV, etc. are not going to elicit the employer's interest in you. Create a picture of you living life to the full outside of your working life. Outdoors activities? Painting portraits? Artisan baking? Many people just fill this section in minimally, thinking that it is not important. In actual fact, this is where you get to show your colourful personality and *joie de vivre*.

### Additional information:
* For example if you any other language(s) you speak, any hobbies you have that contribute useful skills for this job. It actually is important to list hobbies and interests – a) so that the company knows that you have a personality outside of work, and b) to see if you'll mix easily with the team.

### Referees:
* List the names, work postal addresses, phone numbers and email addresses of two referees who know your work well.

# ACADEMIC CV/RESUME TEMPLATE

So the commercial sector has a standard two page format for a CV/ Resume, but applications for academic jobs use a slightly longer format. The reason for this is that the applicant can list the conferences she has attended, any books or papers that have been published, and any other accolades such as 'reader in residence.' A CV/Resume of around four to five pages, but no more; if your CV/Resume is longer than five pages then remove the oldest conference papers, publications and grant awards and summarize them in one line – just refer to them so that they are present on your CV/Resume. Mainly focus on your most important and recent activity, and have answers prepared for any gaps in your academic career in case you are called for interview, in which case you will more than likely be asked about them.

Here is a sample academic CV/Resume template. If you are going to use this as a basis for your own please remove all the instructions on how to complete each section first.

---

**CURRICULUM VITAE**

**Name**

**(Date of birth)**

**Address (not full address – that can be applied later)**

**Phone:**

**Mobile:**

**Email:**

**Qualifications:**

PhD: title, date and place where received, **supervisor's name/ examiners' names**

---

**Bachelor's and Master's degrees: details of where and what awarded and grade achieved.**

**Any other relevant awards, e.g. teaching qualifications**

**Publications:**

**Monograph**

**Title, place and date of publication**

**Articles/Edited Collections**

**Listed in order (or reverse order) including article title, co-authors if any, place and date of publication.**

**Current Employment and Teaching Experience:**

**Give your job title**

**Course title: list courses you teach on and what your responsibilities are for each, e.g. unit leader,** seminar tutor, essay and exam marker etc.

If you are supervising students' postgraduate research list the titles that you are working on.

**Previous Employment Experience:**
List all previous teaching jobs by university and date.

Then describe the nature of the courses and roles you worked on at that institution.

**Conference Papers Given:**

List in reverse order from the most to the least recent, the date, paper title, conference title and venue of each paper given.

**Competencies and Skills:**

List any other roles that you fulfil as part of your academic job, such as editorship of a journal, administrative roles etc.

**Grants Awarded:**

List in order from most to least recent any funding awards received from internal and external sources, including PhD funding, conference grants and research leave/awards.

**Referee:**

List the names, postal addresses, phone numbers and email addresses of two referees who know your academic work well and/or have observed your teaching.

# SKILLS CV/RESUME TEMPLATE

This type of CV/Resume is becoming increasingly common for senior and managerial positions. On this CV/Resume format you hit the ground running as such, because you detailed your skills on the first section of the CV. You do need to be very specific about working out exactly what your unique assets are. You need to make a list of your previous jobs and the skills that you have gained through them; highlight the ones that gives you the edge and list these first. (This will actually be a good exercise to get you thinking about the best keywords to place in the skills section that will put you ahead of your competitors.

There is no room for glossing or bluffing in this type of CV/ Resume. Every single word on it has to nail down the very best of you on the paper you are printing on. Be sharp also in outlining your skills and responsibilities in your current career, and the experiences you have had in the most recent stages of your career path that have added to your brilliant skill set. So when you start writing, you can create a strong impact by using strong, striking words and keeping your statement short and to the point. (Incidentally, this is how sales marketing works). Here are some examples:

- Determined to develop to a senior management position within the next three years.
- Specialist in x, y, z accounting programme/IT programme or anything else called on your specialist skills.
- A valued team manager
- Organized and time-efficient (in managing your own workload, your team's, or any new projects with tight deadlines)
- Motivated to keep developing and adding to my skills – Progression is an important goal
- Manager
- Director
- Good at planning projects
- A good motivator when a team is challenged by criticism, a tight deadline, or fewer people to work extra hard because their colleagues are off sick (this is just an example – you might be a good motivator or a triathlon team. Now there's an example of boosting morale and using silver words of encouragement to get people going!)

You might be all of these or none – these are just examples of how a statement has extra punch if you put a strong, powerful word at the beginning. So make a list of all of these – think back on your career history and draw two columns. In the first, make a list of what you

15

think are your best skills and abilities. In the second, make a list of what your colleagues and former managers have commended you for. There are usually some attributes that you hadn't noticed about yourself, but others will have greatly appreciated.

**Having gathered your skills and summarized them in a statement:** "A driven project manager and team leader ... ". Take some time to think over on how you will write this. Then on the CV/Resume format, start out by listing your professional ambitions and career aims, and how they relate to the job you are applying for. Doing this gives the employer a chance to see what direction you want to move in. For example, if the company offers good promotion opportunities and you want to be promoted to a more senior position in due time, they will be more likely to invest in you than in someone who just wants a regular routine nine to five job with no promotion goals. So there's an instant match between what you can offer each other in the future; you will provide them with fresh blood in higher management positions, and they will be happy to invest in you to get there. Companies who offer good promotion programmes can have a better reputation, because the group dynamic of the people at the top is dynamic. This means more ideas, more young minds with fresh ideas about what their customers want and what the company can do to keep itself up to date while also building a long-term reputation for excellence. So you see, this CV/Resume is a more targeted way of showing why you want the job, how uniquely suitable you are for it, and what makes you the best person for the job.

Although with this format you mainly focus on your skills, which makes it a more dynamic type of CV/Resume, don't forget that it is important to summarize your educational background and job history at the end of the CV/Resume, because employers will want to see this information too. Also ensure that you provide the names and contact details of two referees – usually on request –which can be included on the CV/Resume.

Name

(Date of birth)

Address (not in full until requested)

Phone:

Mobile:

Email:

**Personal Statement**

In a few sentences summarize your career achievements to

date and where you want to go from here (managed, promoted, employee of the year, etc.)

You are basically saying "This is what I have been so far, this is what I want in the future, and this is how I am a match for your job description."

**Skills**

This is where you write a statement about yourself, showing

everything that you can offer to the company. You are basically saying: "This is me, this is what I am excellent at." Then list each skill, give examples and describe any positive outcomes.

**Communication**

* Give examples from your work life, education or personal life that illustrate having good communications skills

**Planning/Organizing**

* Give examples of your experience on project planning or any other project that required you to have excellent planning and organizing skills.

**Teamwork**

* Give examples from your career history of using good teamwork skills and when particularly positive results were earned because of how well the team worked together.

## Training

* Give examples of times when you were involved in training others. You can link the public speaking element back to 'communication.'

## Computing

* List your computer knowledge and skills including the programmes that you have experience using. And so on ... the above are just examples. List your skills and give some of the best examples and outcomes.

## Education and Qualifications

List undergraduate, postgraduate degrees and professional qualifications, institutions, dates and grades awarded. (This section doesn't form the main bulk of a Skills CV/Resume, so

go large with the first three sections and keep education, qualifications and work experience relevant but without going into too much detail. If they want to know more they will ask you in the interview.

## Work Experience

In order of most recent first, list the jobs you have had including company/institution name, position held and dates

## Additional Information

Any other relevant information such as languages spoken, first aider, etc.

## Referees

List the names, work addresses, phone numbers and email addresses of two referees who know your work well.

# CLASSIC CV/RESUME TEMPLATE

This CV/Resume template can be used when applying for several similar jobs. It is the only CV/Resume that you can use generically to post to similar job applications, as long as you tweak it so that it addresses some specific requirements or details about the company you are applying to. It is the most common type of CV/Resume that is in use today. This type is most useful when applying for a job that is similar to one you have already done, and this is why it is easy to update to apply for other similar jobs. By using it you can show that you have the employment-based experience and the qualifications to be an ideal candidate for the job you have applied for.

The personal profile is an important part of this CV/Resume. You need to explain where your career experience has taken you to so far, what skills you have developed along the way, and what your ambition is for your next job. Keep it short and to the point, perhaps only a few sentences. Start by listing your career aims, and then say what makes you the best person for the job.

Go on to list your job history and education in reverse chronological order and go large on the details about what you have gained in your most recent jobs. List your responsibilities alongside your skills, showing how each skill enabled you to meet each responsibility. Describe the context and outcomes of your responsibilities when you relate them to specific achievements in previous jobs. Finally, it is important to remember to give the names and contact details of two referees as well, who will usually be contacted on request.

# THE COVER LETTER

### *Why do you need it, how do you write it? Where do you write it? Where do you send it?*

Having covered all of your best bases in your CV/Resume, writing a cover letter can be confusing. Logically, you can completely forgive yourself for thinking "What? But I've said all this already in my application!" The cover letter is vital because it is an invitation to go to the real event – reading your CV/Resume. Your cover letter is an opportunity to explain why you are applying for this specific job, what you can offer to the company, and how it fits into your career path. It's like a short summary of what you put in your CV/Resume, but written as a personal address to the company you are applying to. It should leave the employer want to read more about you.

If you are emailing your application to the recruiter, put your cover letter as the body of your email. Obviously, if you are snail-mailing your application as a hard copy, write the cover letter on headed paper, including your address and the date, with your name underneath your signature at the end. On the whole, HR directors tend to produce good quality CV/Resumes because they have a lot of experience and understanding of what employers look out for. But I still recommend getting someone else to review it in order to see if it clearly conveys what you have done, where your core competencies lie, and that you have included your most valuable and unique attributes (that match the job you are applying for).

**So again, you need to emphasize your skills in relation to the employer's requirements. Your cover letter is the first thing a recruiter will see, so it is essential that you introduce your CV/Resume and explain why you are best suited for the role and should be invited to an interview. Remember to use those sharp power words that boldly state your best attributes. It's best to format your covering letter as a plain text so that it can be read by any email reader. You could also add it as an attachment to your email application in the form of an A4 page letter so that it is presentable if they print it off.**

*Here are some points about 'cover letter etiquette':*
* Emails are not as easy to read as letters.
* Stick to simple text with short paragraphs and plenty of spacing.
* Break messages into points and make each one a new paragraph with a full line gap between paragraphs.
* DON'T WRITE IN UPPER CASE! NO MATTER WHAT YOU HAVE TO SAY! IT COMES ACROSS AS SHOUTING!

# SO NOW YOU ARE ALL READY TO GO!

If the job application is returnable by email, send your CV/Resume as an attachment, and place your cover letter in the main body of the email as well as attaching it in the format of a letter. Give your assurance to the recruiter that you will also send a printed application package if they require hard copies of your application documents.

It is worth your while getting to know some different document formats. Word is the easiest to use but there are so many versions that it would be easy to send your attachments to someone who has a newer or older version of Word, and therefore can't open them. PDF (Portable Document Format) is becoming one of the most widely used formats. There are PDF readers for all platforms (Windows, Mac OS, Linux).

Something to moan about when emailing a job application is that the platform it is received on could distort the layout of your text. Sometimes all of the paragraph spaces can be squashed together. Other times, the text appears in a single left hand column in ridiculously small font size. So using PDF, which has a very attractive presentation, also guarantees that your CV/Resume will have the same presentation regardless of what platform the reader uses to view the document. Modern versions of Microsoft Word contain a PDF export function or you can download a free pdf converter such as:

'Cutepdf':www.cutepdf.com/Products/CutePDF/writer.asp.

You just follow the instructions to install it and then "print" the document to a folder on your PC.

If you do use MS Word (.doc) format, just keep in mind that it is not guaranteed to be compatible among different versions of Word, so a CV/Resume might look garbled when opened with an outdated or newer version of Word. Also .doc files may not easily open on computers using Linux and Apple platforms. .doc-files may also contain sensitive information such as previous draft versions of a document, which would be highly embarrassing. MS Word documents can contain macro viruses, so some employers may not open these. If you have IT phobia and word is all you can managed, send the CV/Resume in .doc (Word

2003) format, rather than .docx (Word 2010) format, as not everyone has upgraded to Word 2010 or downloaded the free file converter.

You can always call up HR and ask them what platform they use, and what format the documents need to be in. If you are really confused, it might be best to do this first because it could save you a lot of time. If in doubt send your CV/Resume in several formats. Email them all to yourself first to make sure that no embarrassing glitches have happened to your text!

## WHEN TO GET CREATIVE WITH YOUR CV/ RESUME AND WHEN TO KEEP IT PLAIN?

Most career coaches advise keeping your CV/Resume as plain as possible, with only the text needed to say what you need to say. Some companies find a more creative approach impressive. Pixar, the animated movie giant, give their designers access to a playroom to use during breaks and lunchtimes. Yes, a real playroom! The reason for this is that Pixar believe in giving their employees a break from reality to go into a space that fosters creative play, which results in creative thinking. Think around the job you are applying for; most non-creative industries will expect a well-presented CV/Resume, easy to read, not crowded with text, with details given only when relevant. They won't appreciate you adding a background design because they are not assessing your design skills. It could even give them the impression that you like to doodle, and that all of your documents are going to be a bit zany. (And what would their customers think of that?!)

These key 'formal' features of your CV/Resume must be exactly the same if you opt for a more creative design. Some recruiters for design jobs will appreciate a more creative dynamic CV/Resume, but it must still be all about how easy the text is to read. Using a creative style will show off your creative abilities, and employers in media, arts and design often see that as confidence on your part, which will attract them. Ultimately however, the CV/Resume needs to show you off. Whatever you choose, keep formatting consistent and make sure your text font is an appropriate style and size – essentially it must be easy to read.

**Some examples of the 'wrong' kind of CV/Resume**

CV/Resumes have arrived onto recruiters' desks and been consigned straight to the dustbin for the following reasons:

- Coffee/tea stains all over the CV/Resume (evidence of a late night last minute compilation)
- A family holiday snap attached, showing the applicant belly-flopping into a swimming pool ... apparently to show the company that he is 'a good bit of fun.'
- Handprints of food or dusts all over the back of your CV.
- Chocolate stains all over it – you munched your w a y through the panic of getting your application right
- A landscape water colour included as evidence of the applicant's passion for environmental issues (listed in her hobbies and interests)
- A receipt for postage attached with a request for reimbursement
- An extra page requesting help – the applicant states that he feels like a loser, can't get any job   he is looking for and can the recruiter coach him or give him feedback?
- An invitation to meet for lunch the day before the interview
- Writing "BIG LOVE" at the end of the cover letter
- Writing "I LOVE WHAT YOU GUYS DO!" instead of "I want to work for your company because ..."

So if you don't mess up that bad you're in with a good chance with your application!

# SHOULD I INCLUDE A THUMBNAIL PHOTO OF MYSELF?

The short answer to this is, 'only if you are requested to' (this is commonly used in some part of US). Brains respond to faces unconsciously before they consciously respond to text, and thumbnails tend to flatten your personality and make your natural expressions a bit restrained. None of us would put a passport photo onto a CV/Resume, so hold back your image until you get called for interview, then you can groom and shine! Anyway, it's not really appropriate to beam a great smile for a formal thumbnail photograph, so what happens instead is that by not smiling, the face looks threating.

## GETTING THE TONE RIGHT

The most important thing to remember is 'CHP' – be Concise, Honest and Positive:

- **Concise** – don't use unnecessary words, don't use too many adjectives, and don't ramble in your application.
- **Honest** – whether you are playing down your qualifications to get a less senior position, or playing up your qualifications to get to a more senior position, you will be found out. If an employer is interested in you she will check everything on your CV/Resume – previous companies, universities, etc. And please do ensure that your referees actually exist!
- **Positive** – even if promotion is not important to you and you just want a job to support your income needs, be positive and ambitious. By doing this you give out the right energy and come across as being enthusiastic and up to the challenge.

You do not have to disclose every employment disaster in your CV/Resume. Remember you need to sparkle off the page and dazzle the recruiter. A CV/Resume is not an appropriate place to complain about previous jobs, or to show any sense of self-doubt or lack of self-esteem.

## GAPS IN MY CAREER HISTORY

First, take a deep breath and calm down. We all have them – life simply gets in the way of giving 40 hours per week to an employer. Think well in advance of writing how you are going to explain any gaps in your CV/Resume, so that you don't end up fumbling some last minute answers. For young people, travel and gap years are to be expected so that explains that. For older people the gaps could be due to anything from illness, childcare, caring for an elderly relative, or living the dream of volunteering abroad (in which case you have probably taken a career break). You may have had some extra cash so you took some time off to spend more quality time at home with your family. Voluntary work experience whether internationally or locally are an admirable, credible way to explain any gaps. One word of warning though: don't invent any untrue stories. Your recruiter has plenty of opportunity to check up on your background. You don't want to be noted as being dishonest before you even make it to the interview chair. In fact, you won't even make it past the front door.

## Case study: long gap in employment.

*Even as a student, Amaka had momentous drive and ambition to earn the opportunities to do what she was most good at. She had built up an impressive CV/Resume of experience before she graduated from university. She was involved in volunteering in projects that provided stimulation and activities for the less privileged, she had worked with a young people's charity to build a healthy community, and she had worked part-time as a proof-reader and editor. She also had two years of teaching under her belt.*

*This experience meant that she had a whole portfolio of skills to put forward when it came to applying for jobs. She had worked with young and old people, and had managed clients in an entrepreneurial sense through her proof-reading and editing work.*

*She continued working part-time while she pursued philosophy – her dream subject – at university, all the way to PhD level. So after she graduated she had an extensive record of employment and a queue of referees who were fighting with each other over who got to provide the first reference.*

*She applied for a senior position with a voluntary sector charity – to manage a team of support workers and volunteers, and to manage any difficult situations with their service users. Her application was snapped up and she was invited to an interview straightaway. To cut a long story short, she was offered the position and started work three weeks later.*

*She loved it initially but found after the first three months that she was battling with her energy levels and getting the flu a lot. As time went on she had various tests carried out, and when every other possibility had been eliminated she was diagnosed with M.E. (commonly known as Chronic Fatigue Syndrome or Chronic Fatigue Immune Deficiency Syndrome). She ate a healthy diet anyway and didn't burn the candle at both ends, so she decided to continue working until it really began to become a problem. Almost a year later she came down with another debilitating flu and this time couldn't pull out of it. She knew that she couldn't return to work.*

*As anyone who suffers with this condition knows, when it is at its peak the sufferer has no option but to put life down into the lowest gear and stop pretty much everything, so that the body can rest and heal. Doing too much sets it all off again, back to square one. With M.E. there is pain all over the body, flu, fever, a feeling of the brain being on fire, and weakness to the point where it's difficult to get from room to room.*

*All the time in the background Amaka had a gnawing anxiety about what was going to happen to her employment history on a CV. This employment gap could potentially last three, even five years or more. Of course, the sufferer can work out some kind of way of working from home on a part-time basis to keep up their professional skills and give a boost to their self-esteem.*

But when it's time to return to work and apply for a full-time job, there's a big dilemma here. It's natural to worry that if you apply for a job and have not worked for, let's say, five years, that's a big chunk of time to explain. And if the explanation is that you have suffered with a chronic illness that can have lifelong effects, how likely are they to employ you?

"Illness" always looks worse on paper than it does on the face and personality of the applicant, so at least wait for that opportunity to speak about it face-to-face. Understandably, the employer will want to ask you how you are likely to deteriorate within a space of time of having settled into the job. Again, a long-term illness is a disability, so you can negotiate with them some changes that they could make for you. This could include:

Making your timetable flexible so that you can stay on and work hard when you feel well, in balance with finishing early when you don't feel 100%

- Most companies should provide a staff restroom; a quiet room, away from the kitchen, where staff-members can go in and have a quiet 15 minutes
- Some kind of flexibility around when you take your annual leave. If you feel that it would be of benefit to be able to 'recover' on time when you need to recharge your batteries, it's the perfect idea
- An office of your own so you don't become overloaded by phones ringing, the babble of staff laughing and chatting, and all the other office noises that either drive you crazy or you become immune to
- Regular supervision meetings with your manager so that you can discuss your workload, how you are pacing it, how you are pacing yourself, and if this is working for both parties

If you have a gap in your career because of illness or redundancy, here are some examples of what you can say you did to make your time productive:

- Volunteered with a local charity This means that you can keep your CV/Resume up to date, and progress to more senior volunteer positions.
- Set up and ran a community project (to create a youth center, for example)

This shows that you are aware of problems, and driven to find a solution and put it into action. Also, if you can work across the community you can work comfortably with a diverse range of people

- Gradually set up your own business (it could be freelance writing, event management and interior decorations, or anything else)

This shows huge entrepreneurial spirit and drive to continue developing your professional abilities even when you have to spend a long time at home because of illness.

- Following training from 'X' national support group, you raised funds and attracted sponsorship to run a part-time help-line to support other people with the same condition as you Jackpot! You raised funds to set up a charitable service, which you ran part-time by yourself.
- Ran a home-baked bread cake stall at your local market

Well I defy anyone to knock this one. It shows good time management (if because you had to have everything prepared and be at the market between fixed hours). And the simplicity of the product is actually a commodity that many people will pay large money for, because who has the time anymore to wait for their loaf of bread to prove, or beat in enough air to make their Victoria sponge light and fluffy? Entrepreneurial drive, artisan production and organized partnership (with the market times and rules).

You can add anymore that you can think of. And don't forget to include the highpoints of your previous employments on your CV/Resume. If you have been travelling, talk about how different experiences really challenged your character to mature and develop. If you've had to care for someone who was sick or elderly, talk about how difficult the role of the career is. It is physically hard work, it often means not being able to sleep through the night so you have to be extra-organized and have plenty of tricks up your sleeve for alternative ways to manage your time. In terms of communication, you are likely to be in contact with the person's entire care team – GP, social worker, occupational therapist, hospital consultant, community nurse, and so on. Communicating with this range of people, who have such different roles, is a challenge to how effectively you can both remain confident to be yourself, but switch to a more formal, professional tone of conversation when you need to. Just remember that if you have to explain a gap in your career history, explain it in the best possible light. The main message you want to give is that *you have continued to develop your skills and competencies, and developed new ones.*

# LET'S RECAP: TIPS ON PRESENTING YOUR CV/RESUME

If I've overloaded you with information so far, just have a breather here and make a mental note to commit the following tips to memory.

- Your CV/Resume should be **carefully and clearly laid out** – not too cramped but not patchy with large empty spaces either. Use bold and italic typefaces for headings and important information.

- **Never 'backpage'** a CV/Resume - each page should be on a separate sheet of paper. It's a good idea to put your name in the footer area so that it appears on each sheet, and to number each page.

- **Be concise:** a CV/Resume is an appetizer (speed date!) and should not give the reader indigestion. Don't feel that you have to list every exam you have ever taken, or every activity you have ever been involved in. Just consider which are the most relevant and/or impressive. The best CV/Resumes tend to be fairly economical with words, selecting the most important information and leaving a little something for the interview: they are an appetizer rather than the main course. Good business communications tend to be short and to the point, focusing on key facts and your CV/Resume should to some extent emulate this.

- **Be positive** - put yourself over confidently (but n o t as being over-confident or arrogant), in your CV/Resume or in your interview, and highlight your strong points. For example, when listing your A levels, put your highest grade first.

- **Be honest:** although a CV/Resume does allow you to omit details (such as exam re-sits) which you would prefer the employer not to know about, you should never give inaccurate or misleading information. Okay, CVs/Resumes are not legal documents and you can't be held liable for anything within, but if a recruiter picks up a suggestion of falsehoods you will be rapidly rejected.

- **Choose a sensible email address**, preferably your name and surname at whatever network you use. Don't provide an email address with your date of birth in it such as Susie77@gnumail. com ; keep your own personal privacy safe until you've got the job or at least been shortlisted for interview, at which point it is more appropriate to provide these details. By every means possible avoid email addresses like : s e x y l i k e w o a a a a h @ h o t m i l k . c o m , y o u r m y w i f e n o w @ g n u m a i l . c o m, so_kiss_me@hotmilk.com, etc. Bear in mind that interviewers/ employers have hundreds of CV/Resumes on their desk to go through and email addresses like the examples above portray you as being irresponsible, unserious and unreliable. They show a lack of respect for the company you are applying to.

- **Your email address alone can 'speak' badly of you,** resulting in it being dashed before the recruiter even reads below your personal details. Remember that every employer wants to recruit someone who is mature and who can represent their company to clients, suppliers, stakeholders, and so on. It doesn't matter if you act like a 12 year old at home; just don't let your potential employer get a whiff of you being anything but professional and competence

- **Create your profile:** keywords and work experience from the present backwards. Do likewise with education, awards and training/other qualifications. Information about volunteering is important (if it's relevant to what you are applying for). Hobbies and interests give the employer an idea of who you are behind your professional role. A prospective boss might love the fact that you are a Formula 1 enthusiast.

- Give the names, work addresses, phone numbers, email addresses of **two referees,** stating their professional relationship to you or you can leave it out but provide it on request (clearly state it on your CV though).

- **Highlight any leadership positions** you have held by locating them in a prominent position o n y o u r CV/Resume and using the words 'led' 'managed' 'supervised' 'oversaw' 'team leader' or whatever else you feel is appropriate.

- **Showcase your 'extra attributes'** – see what you can find out about the company director or who will be on the interview panel(LinkedIn is often the easiest route)
- How to **make your hobbies and interests relevant:** E.g., if you are interested in environmental issues and are applying for a job in archaeology or outdoor community development, these are an obvious perfect match. Out of the ordinary hobbies show a sense of adventure and strong people skills if the job involves teaming up with other people, please don't go on blabbing how you like watching African magic from morning to night (which a lot of people do). Just keep that to yourself.
- Use **keywords** associated with that sector, and corporate terms such as 'blue sky thinking,' 'lateral thinking' 'synergy (between associates/business partners)', etc.
- Show that you have a **sociable personality and good people skills**. From your work experience, highlight the areas where you had to deal with people and describe some interesting ways that you socialize with others. It will impress them too if you say that you don't judge people on first impressions because you have met people in the past and disliked them, only to go on and set up a part- time business with them, (or whatever your own example is).

## BREAKING IT DOWN AND MAKING SENSE.

So you've got all the pointers, and it's taken 2 ½ chapters to get here. The question now is how you can distil everything you have learned down to the most important elements. If you remember these, they will form the centre-point of your CV/Resume and will guide you in everything else you have to write.

## These are the fundamentals of CV/Resume writing:

- **Profile** (this is where you outline your Unique Selling Proposition)
- **Keywords** – outline your competencies, making them as specific as possible
- **Work Experience and responsibilities** (use action words)
- **Education/Qualifications** (highlighting your best results)
- **Awards/training/achievements** – it's easy to forget these, so make sure to keep all of your certificates in one place.
- **Hobbies and interests** – describe them in such a way that they reveal more about your winning personality!
- **2 referees** – make sure you left them on good terms and that they can give an accurate picture of your skills and employment attributes.

### Some wrong examples

- \* **Profile:** although I used the analogy of speed-dating and online dating to explain how we first connect with an employer, please do not write your profile like a 'Meet a Partner' column.
  *Available for companionship; interested in both men and women, and experimenting with new experiences. A true intellectual at heart, I can talk to you about Sartre for hours.*

The equivalent on a CV/Resume could be something like:
*Average person seeks work to improve social life and get out of the house more, and maybe meet the girl of my dreams ...*

- \* **Keywords:** words such as these are not likely to inspire any potential recruiter – funny, the office clown, laid back, school prefect in Year 1 ...

If you look back at our CV/Resume templates you will find discussions of the best types of keywords to use and how to match them to your experience so that how you use them looks natural.

**Work experience**

When talking about your work experience take care to organize what you did into verbs (action words) first.

Examples of action words are:

- I developed
- I planned
- I led
- I achieved ...
- I negotiated (for an x% reduction from two of our suppliers)
- I managed (a team of 'y' people)

Whatever work you have done previously, be it working in a restaurant, a shop, or delivering conflict resolution training, spell out the relevant details. Make sure that your prospective employer knows the key strengths of your role in your previous relevant jobs. If you have worked on the front line of customer service and as part of a team, highlight how you provided quality service to customers, tactfully dealt with complaints, and how you contributed to team cooperation. You don't have to explain the more mundane aspects of your daily routine, especially non-people tasks (such as cleaning tables or toilets if you worked in hospitality or as a cleaner) on your CV/Resume.

The only exception is if you are applying for something related to it. That brings us back around to that key point again -- when talking about your work experience you should always try to relate the old to the job you are applying for. For example, a finance job will involve Numeracy, Analytical and Problem Solving skills. If you are applying for a marketing role, you need to place more emphasis on communication, engaging people, and using persuasion and negotiation to excel in this role. So how do you think you would relate these two? First off, it's not a good idea to apply for a job that you have no experience in. But what about this scenario?

*Finance and accounting tend to make the eyes of the uninitiated glaze over when it comes to understanding accounting systems and those endless spread-sheets. If you have worked in finance and have sold a finance package to a client by explaining it in an accessible way for the lay person, that's a form of marketing. You have taken a product (your finance system) and explained how it works, and why it will benefit the client.*

So in that scenario you have sold a pretty obscure product that is essential in one form or another to all businesses. Companies can't run efficiently without having a proper finance system in place to pay suppliers, pay salaries, manage expenses such as fuel for distribution, etc. It is a fairly simple conversion to make; instead of talking about working in finance per se, you shift the focus to how finance is a difficult product to market, and how you managed to introduce a particular system to new clients. You will have used clear explanation, good interpersonal skills (or they would have walked away the moment you mentioned 'finance system'), persuasion (that yours is the particular product that will benefit them most), and negotiation (to negotiate the deal).

So wherever possible, if you can't directly relate a previous job to the one you are applying for, try shifting the focus to a different aspect of what you have done and see if you can bring it in line that way with the job you want.

## HOW TO ARTICULATE YOUR ATTRIBUTES

Here are some examples of how you can use action verbs to frame your statements about your previous work:

- **I increased** a company's sales level as part of a team, which as a result led to the expansion of t h e business by 'z'% and attracted 'x' number o f n e w customers while retaining existing customers and increasing their satisfaction.
- **I provided** efficient and thorough **customer service** by handling their queries and concerns in a professional and supportive manner. Before they left satisfied I always sought to ensure that they felt they could trust my customer service.

# INTERESTS AND ACHIEVEMENTS

By the time you get to this point you will have taken up a lot of your CV/Resume space discussing your work experience, education and qualifications. So make sure to make this section concise but interesting. Think carefully about how you phrase things:

- Instead of 'socializing with friends' say that you do a hobby such as 'going to the movies with friends' or 'motor-biking with friends'. It's better that you do 'something' together rather than 'nothing.'

- Cut down the amount of solitary activities that y o u do. Most people watch TV as a way to unwind – it's not a hobby. Also, too many solitary activities will lead a recruiter to wonder why you spend so much time alone. There's nothing wrong with being the kind of person who enjoys your own company ... just don't advertise that fact on your CV/Resume, b e c a u s e your employer is measuring what you do in your spare time against a criteria of how well you will represent and invigorate the company.

- Making the 'interests and hobbies' section too long is going to appear bogus to the employer – it just looks like you're padding out your CV/Resume to conceal the fact that you don't have much work experience.

- Use bullet points to separate your interests in activities, (sports or anything physically demanding), creativity (writing, world cinema, flower arranging, etc.)

- Volunteering/community work

- Show that you take part in a range of activities to show that you are a well-rounded person. A prospective employer will wonder whether you have substance to your personality if you seem to have no interests outside of work.

- Hobbies that are a little out of the ordinary can help you stand out from the crowd: skydiving or mountaineering can show a sense of wanting to stretch your capabilities have an ability to rely on yourself in demanding situations.

- Any evidence of leadership is important to mention: captain or coach of a sports team, course representative, chair of a student s o c i e t y, scout leader: *"As a football coach of the school football team, I had to set a positive example, motivate and coach players and think on my feet in every situation."*

Finally, when you prioritize your hobbies and interests remember that you can mention anything that shows evidence of employability skills such as team work, organizing, planning, persuasion, negotiation, etc.

## Case Study: why not portraying enough of yourself on your CV is sabotage

*John has an MSc in Mechanical Engineering. He did his undergraduate degree first, then got some reasonably well paid work experience on a new hospital building site, working with one of the project managers. This was enough experience to show him that he was moving in the right direction, and he set his goals on studying further so he could work his way up to becoming a project manager. After that, there would be no limitations on where he could work, or on what projects – mechanical engineering involves a lot of large scale construction design such as airports and large industrial parks.*

*So John worked and saved, and when he had enough money to get through his part-time Masters Degree with a part-time job on the side, he went back to university. In the meantime, he married his girlfriend Jessica, who worked in hospitality. They would often tease each other that he was responsible for running a tight ship while a hotel was being built, then she would step in and take over as captain when the hotel opened for business.*

*He graduated with a distinction and started to apply for jobs straightaway. He was shortlisted for interview for about 30% of the jobs he applied for, but for some reason that he couldn't understand, he wasn't being offered anything after he attended the interview. His academic results and his practical work experience gave him an impeccable track record for the job, and he had expected to throw himself headlong into the first attractive offer he received.*

*So what was going on with John? His CV was too full of skills and abilities not to invite him to an interview, but the interviewers had reservations about whether he had the kind of well-rounded personality that he would need to fit in well with his new team. What we know is that John worked like a Trojan for all of his achievements. When he wasn't studying he was working part-time and saving up for his wedding.*

*He had no problem answering questions about his qualifications or about mechanical engineering in general. He had no apprehensions about working on huge construction projects, or on-site maintenance with a large commercial building that housed some high profile businesses. But when it came to talking about himself, he dried up. He couldn't think of what makes him laugh and he had no recent hobbies or interests to get involved in during his spare time. To be fair, it wasn't Johns' fault – he just didn't have any spare time. All that the interviewers could see was that his interview confirmed their reservations about his CV/Resume. His application showed someone highly skilled but boring, and he wasn't able to portray himself in an interesting light at the interview, so again, they considered him to be 'boring.'*

We don't know John; he's probably far too boring. But his interview preparation focused on the work related questions – the serious stuff. So did his CV/Resume. And he just couldn't think of anything to say when the interviewers said *"Tell us something interesting about yourself, anything at all."*

How do you clinch the interview if you have the same problem? As part of your interview preparation spend some time hanging out with friends doing recreational things, nothing to do with work. Go to the cinema, go climbing, watch a box-set of DVDs to catch up on that series you missed. You might find out on LinkedIn or wherever you research your interviewers that one of them studied forensic psychology – tell them you're addicted to crime dramas. (If you don't know of any, find someone who does and get them to talk you through the main characters and some of the most eventful episodes). Do the same with anything you are going to state as being one of your interests and hobbies – know enough facts about it so that you can 'link' with one or more of the interviewers on a relaxed subject.

We know that John hadn't done this. Instead of coming across as a blank personality, he could have said:

*"In the past I used to play tennis every Saturday and go climbing on Sundays. After work in the evening, ideally I love to just chill out with some good TV, or an easy-going book with some music on. But I've had to work so hard to earn my Masters, get married and provide plenty of money for us to live on, that these fell by the wayside for a while. I love letting my mind switch off and totally focus on something else, so I can't wait to get back to doing relaxing things once I get back into a regular work routine. It'll be easier when I have one full-time job rather than fitting in lots of part-time jobs, which is what I'm doing at the moment. I can't wait to start work with a new time and discover some new interests through them. I'm always up for doing something new."*

This shows that he's an adventurous kind of guy who can switch off from work completely to wind down, and he can form friendships easily. Like many professionals at the moment, he is working lots of part-time hours because in the current economy firms are somewhat reluctant to offer fulltime, permanent contracts. This is a positive answer that explains how he feels "stuck" at the moment but he's poised and ready to leap back into doing all the fun things in his life again. To round himself out even more to the interviewers he could add some details about his experiences doing voluntary work or taking part in university societies.

### *Describing your extra-curricular self is as important as describing your professional self. Be well prepared!*
**Another typical example;**

Joyce was invited for an interview after series of rejections and disappointments, one of the interviewers on the panel asked Joyce what she would do if her boss (that is married) was hitting on her (i.e. if her boss was asking her out) her response was appalling but understandable. This was her response;

"If my boss tries that rubbish, I will give it to him (tell him off)" with such a serious expression on her face and a bit of attitude. Of course she dint get that job because your potential employer will be there thinking that this lady can't handle or work under pressure and can easily flip with any little discomfort or disturbance.

Now I do understand that it can be very annoying being pestered by your boss especially a married one for that matter, this is what she could have said "I will politely make him understand that my principles and believes don't promote such but will say it in a respectful and professional manner and from that point will try to avoid him as much as I can and also watch how I dress to work". That way, you are not disrespecting or insulting anyone, this answer simply shows that you can handle issues in a respectful and mature way.

## TARGETING YOUR CV/RESUME

I've mentioned this once or twice already, but there's no limit on how many times I give you this advice: target your CV/Resume towards every job. Even when you use the Classic CV/Resume format which you can complete for several similar job applications, still make a few changes that individualize each one. In the present competitive job market, undirected CV/Resumes tend to lose out to those that have been written with a particular role in mind. For example, a marketing CV/Resume will be very different from a teaching CV/Resume. The marketing CV/Resume will focus on persuading, negotiating and similar skills whereas the teaching CV/Resume will focus more on presenting and listening skills and evidence for these.

Even if you are using the same CV/Resume for a number of employers (though even still, you'll find ways to tweak and individualize each one), you should also tailor or personalize the covering letter by including a paragraph on why you want to work for that particular organization, for example. Their values may align with your own, or you've found through research that the head of the company has received accolades for his/her ability to support staff and encourage them to work to their full potential.

# DISABILITIES – SHOULD I DISCLOSE IN A CV/RESUME?

Firstly, you are not required to do so by law, so it is a purely personal decision. There is usually an equal opportunities form included with your job application pack which states that anything you write on it is kept confidential from your recruiter (Not all organizations though). If your disability causes you to need extra time for written assessments or means that you need special adjustments made to the environment to maximize your mobility, then you're best to go ahead and explain this on the application. It means that you make it easier for yourself on the day of the interview.

Most people hear a medical term and conjure the worst picture imaginable. Try to keep away from medical labels for your disability and think of a phrase that explains how it affects you physically but also shows off your strengths. In other words, you can disclose your disability and cast yourself in a positive light. Something like:

*Spent two years in a wheelchair following car accident but now walk comfortable indoor distances on one crutch.*

Explaining your disability in a way that shows off your determination to lead as unimpeded a life as possible shows immense strength and drive to move forward in your life. If your disability is mental health related but well-controlled with the help of therapies and medication, you might feel more comfortable thinking of it as 'dormant' at the moment. The same with chronic illnesses such as Chronic Fatigue Syndrome, Fibromyalgia and M.E.; if they are 'dormant' or not in flare-up when you are applying for the job they might become a problem again in the future but for now, you are applying as someone who is fit for work and capable of doing the job. Again, you can describe it in a phrase that casts you in a positive light:

*By following a special diet and healthy lifestyle I have brought my energy levels and physical ability back up to 9 (or 10) again after a long period of illness.*

You might want to elaborate and say that you had to become expert in your own recovery so you recognize the signs of deteriorating again and you know how to respond by changing your daily routine, getting more rest, and so on. If your sickness record is requested on the job application you can explain any long absences but also emphasize that you found some 'work from home' projects to keep up your professional skills and maintain a healthy routine. For any disability, don't mention any adjustments that your employer would need to make for you until you have been offered the job.

You can be sure that you've been offered the job on your own merit, and because the employer feels that the company will benefit from having you on board. Having your entrance talk with your supervisor is the best time to raise your disability as an 'any other business' matter – you've been accepted for you, now let the employer know that you can accept them if they make accommodations for your disability. Employment anti-discrimination laws that support people with disabilities in employment mean that you cannot be discriminated against, and if you feel that you are being so, you can report the recruiter. If you feel that it is going to be hard to prove, see who you can call on as an ally.

The main guideline to remember is to be easy with yourself and be realistic about how you can manage your disability within the requirements of the job you are applying for. You may need to be versatile in what you want to do, and may possibly have to reject one or two job offers before you find one that suits your career ambitions and accommodates your disability. It's not about imposing limitations on yourself – the opposite: it's about working within your range of capabilities in order to secure the perfect job.

**Special Focus: Applying for jobs if you have a disability** A disability is loosely defined as being a physical or mental condition that has a noticeable impact on an individual's ability to do what other people would consider as 'normal' daily activities. This might include looking after personal hygiene and cooking food, getting through the day without feeling anxious, spend a whole day at work, or be able to take part in a choice of extra-curricular activities. A disability is defined if the symptoms are present for more than one year.

Discrimination laws are similar in the UK and the US, though you will have to check the specifics of whichever country you live in. Typically, recognized disabilities include: speech, language and learning difficulties such as:

- Dyslexia
- Dyspraxia
- Dyscalculia
- AD(H)D (Attention Deficit Hyperactivity Disorder
- Asperger's Syndrome

## Mental and emotional difficulties such as:

- Depression
- Anxiety
- Psychosis
- Schizophrenia
- Eating disorders

Physical disabilities are too numerous to list here, but again, check with your national department of health to see where you fit in.
Visual and hearing impairments:

- Full or partial blindness
- Full or partial deafness
- And other impairments

## Chronic medical conditions such as:

- Heart disease
- Stroke
- Emphysema and other chest problems
- M.E./ Chronic Fatigue Syndrome
- Cancer
- Diabetes

This is nowhere near a complete list, but it gives you an idea of the categories of disability. Employers cannot dismiss a job application solely on the grounds of the applicant having a disability. They also have no right to ask you about a disability unless they want to offer you the job, in which case you disclose your disability in a positive light, in the context of what you can do and what, if any, adjustments they need to make for you.

What they can do is to ask you about your disability during recruitment to make sure that you can move on to the next stage, or if they need to make any adjustments early on in the recruitment process. If there are particular tasks that are specific to the role, they might want to check with you beforehand. This makes sense – if you can't do the task, it would be a waste of your time and theirs to attend an interview. Also, they might want to check out whether they need to register you with occupational therapy.

Once an employer has offered you the job they have to cooperate fully with Occupational health and ensure that whatever adjustments (within reason) are required are carried out. They need to promote a culture of equality in the workplace, and offer uncompromised support if disabled staff are being harassed.

## REASONS WHY YOU MIGHT FIND IT USEFUL TO DISCLOSE YOUR DISABILITY.

Whether you disclose your disability or not is entirely up to you. If you disclose it and the company turns you away, well you wouldn't have wanted to work with them anyway. Here are some reasons why you might want to disclose your disability during the recruitment process:

- You might need to have the law on your side if you need to be honest about your disability but find that you aren't getting called for interviews.
- You might want to show that you have a 'can do 'attitude by explaining your disability in a positive, empowered way.
- You might be applying to employers who you know to have a positive attitude to hiring staff with a disability.
- You may disclose it on the Equal Opportunities questionnaire.

**Reasons for the employer to find your disclosure useful**

- They can arrange to make extra time for you if need be, or allow you to bring in some notes if you have memory impairment
- There may be some health and safety checks that they need to do to ensure your safety before you come in
- The employers might have collected all Equal

Opportunities questionnaires from the recruiter to see if anyone has a disability (this doesn't always happen but it can sometimes). You may feel better about having been up front from the beginning, and they are more likely to respect you (if they are decent human being that is!) for not viewing it as a negative aspect and trying to hide it.

But then, many recruiters are not decent human beings, and you might instinctively have your guard up because you fear that your disclosure won't be respected. It is perfectly normal to fear being discriminated against or placed in a category before the person making this judgement has even met you. If you do get the job you may fear being labelled before you even get your foot in the door on day one. Also, from a pragmatic point of view, if you know that your disability is entirely unrelated to your ability to do the job, then no-one at your workplace has any right to know (unless they still need to make some adjustments for you).

**When's the best time to disclose?**

How long is a piece of string! Here are some options for you; you'll probably recognize what stage you're at:

1. Straight off on your application – you can disclose it but as a feature of you describing your strengths and how you strive to get on in life regardless of your disability
2. Anonymously on the Equal Opportunities monitoring questionnaire
3. When you write your covering letter, which you will tailor to the job

4. When you arrive at the interview venue; or you might phone up the company in advance and ask to speak with one of the interviewers so that they know on the day.

5. Or you can decide not to disclose it until you a) are offered the job, or b) have started your job

**Here are some examples of well-worded disclosures:**

*"When I started university I had to learn how to organize myself and manage my time so that I had extra room for learning things and going over them again.*

*I have worked out two reliable strategies for processing thoughts and information that means my short term memory deficit is no longer a problem."*

The European Ministerial Conference on Mental Health (World Health Organization 2005) links every type of health to mental health. Whether your disability is a physical or mental illness, your employer should make you feel as supported as possible, so that going to work is enjoyable and not an ordeal that makes you feel anxious about managing your physical or emotional symptoms.

Here's a powerful quote from the conference:

*There is no health without mental health. Mental health is central to the human, social and economic capital of nations and should therefore be considered as an integral and essential part of other public policy areas such as human rights, social care, education and employment.*

With that as your backing, you'll get off to a powerful start in any job you are offered!

# Chapter 3:

# INTERVIEWS – PREPARATION AND PERFORMANCE

So you've been shortlisted for interview – that means that you're far more than halfway there!

The key to maintaining a positive mental attitude to your interview is to believe that if the recruiters want to meet you, you've as good as got the job in the bag. They've read your CV/Resume and your cover letter, they're satisfied that you are really interested in working for them; now they want to interview you to confirm their first impressions about you. All you need to do now is prepare properly so that all of your answers are tailored towards confirming their impressions.

The 'Interviews – Preparation and Research' section of this book gives you some comprehensive advice on how to cope with the predictable and unpredictable questions that are frequently asked by interviewers. Let's just do a quick spot-check first. If you still find that you are not being invited to attend interviews, checking your application against the following tips will help:

- **Revise your CV/Resume:** As we discussed earlier in this book, one of the single biggest mistakes most job applicants make is to send the same CV/Resume to every single job application. You must tailor your CV/Resume to suit each application depending on what company you are applying to, what position, and which skills are required. For instance, if you are applying for a customer service role, ensure to draw out your experience with customers or even as a student if you have not worked in a more professional capacity as a customer service assistant before.

- **Get a second opinion:** Getting a second opinion goes a long way to helping you to secure that all-important job interview. After you have drafted your CV/Resume, pass it around to get as many opinions on it as possible. It would be wise to ask a friend, a teacher/university professor or a trusted colleague for constructive comments. This will enable you spot one or two mistakes and suggest possible ways of making it better.

- **Gain more of the right experience:** The challenge with so many people applying for jobs today is the lack of requisite experience compared to competitors. The most effective way around this is for you to volunteer to work first as an unpaid intern and then to consequently gather work experience for at least six months, possibly in your dream work place. This shows the recruiter that you really want to work in this area; someone who wasn't so keen probably wouldn't spend six months gaining work experience without being paid. I'm taking from experience, I remember back then when I was done with university and was out there in the job market, after months of rejections due to lack of relevant experience, I had to opt for an unpaid internship (which I did for almost a year), well, I was only paid a stipend which could barely cover my transportation and feeding and was nothing compared to the kind of responsibilities I was given. But hey it paid off at last because now I can confidently apply for any job in line with the experience I gained. Gaining work experience will help you to understand the area from the inside out and pick its day to day runnings. Doing this will boost your confidence, expand your skills and increase the probability that you may be retained at the end of your internship. (You may still have to attend an internal interview to move up to a higher position, so keep reading!). Also, you will know what you are talking about at an interview, leaving the recruiter with no doubt that this is an area of work that is familiar to you. With these in place, the sky is definitely your starting point.

Having made these checks, let's move on to preparing for the interview itself. Here's a quick-check guide that you can write on a piece of card and keep in your pocket, so you are rarely too far away from thinking about how your preparation is going:

- Research the company
- Find out from HR what type of interview will be conducted
- Study extensively how to prepare for the interview questions
- Find out who will be on the panel if you can
- Practise with friends and in front of a mirror
- If you suffer with anxiety or particular nervousness, work on the stress-relieving exercises given to you in this book
- Dress smartly and go for a formal look rather than anything that draws attention to itself
- Prepare any questions that you want to ask at the end
- Practise how to close the interview confidently and pleasantly
- Ask yourself if you really want this job, or if you would be secretly horrified to be offered it

## RESEARCHING THE COMPANY

It is absolutely a taboo for you to go for an interview without an adequate knowledge of where and who you intend to work for. It is almost like moving into a house without knowing how much the rent is, or how many rooms it has. Most interviewers don't just want people with the right skills and experience; they also want to hire a candidate who is enthusiastic about their organization, the very first interview I ever went for was a nightmare, I naively went for this interview without a thorough research on the company of course when it got to the stage where I was asked about the company, I completely went blank, at that point, I knew that was it. Of course I dint get the job.

One of the ways to prove that you are the best candidate is to thoroughly research about the company or organization. This will enable you to confidently answer any question about the company. More so, it won't only give you a huge plus in how you put your expertise across; it will also show the interviewers how serious you are about working for them.

Most companies will not directly give you any information about them so it is your responsibility to go to their websites, get their catalogues/brochures/annual reports and study as much as your memory can hold about them to enable you to have the most impressive answers at your fingertips. If you can't access these you can call them up to ask one or two questions about them; this will give you an edge over other candidates. Excellent research can make a huge difference between success and failure in this regard. Here is a sketch of the very minimum information you need to know about a company before your interview:

- The goals and objectives of the company
- How many people work for them?
- How many branches they currently have
- How they operate -- locally or internationally?
- Where the head office is
- What services they provide
- When the company was established
- Their mission statement and vision for the future

Here are some more things that you can find out through some general research online or from the employers' customer services or HR department:

- The size of the organization and what its various departments are
- Who'll be on the panel (it is essential to research them)
- The values and ethos of the company (and find examples in your own life that align with these)

# TYPES OF INTERVIEW

Just like there are different CV/Resume formats, different types of company or organization will have a different interviewing style. Here are the main ones to expect:

### Competency-based interviews

Many large graduate recruiters now use competency-based (also called "structured" or "situational") interviews in which the questions are designed to help candidates give evidence of the personal qualities which are needed to perform well in the job. Usually, in reply to these questions, you will be expected to give an example of how you have demonstrated these qualities in the past. You can start preparing now by compiling a list of examples and situations:

### Describe a situation where you had to.....

- show leadership
- make a difficult decision
- work as a member of a team
- use initiative
- change your plans at the last minute
- overcome a difficult obstacle
- refuse to compromise
- work with others to solve a problem

The cons of competency-based or structured interviews are that they can seem unfriendly and off-putting to candidates. They do not give opportunities for discussion - when you have answered one question as far as you feel able, the interviewer will move on to another topic. The advantages of these types of interviews are that they are standardized. This is important when many different interviewers are assessing a large number of graduate applicants. In order for the recruiting and interviewing process to be fair, the standardized questions are based upon the skills essential for the job, and you have the assurance that other competitors are being asked the same thing.

## "Traditional" interviews

These are more like a conversation, but are a conversation with a purpose. Remember to keep up your positive attitude that you are the right person for the job, so bear this in mind when replying to the questions. These interviews will probably be compiled largely from what you say in your application form or CV/Resume, with some curveball questions thrown in to test your ability to think on the spot.

The interviewer may focus on areas of particular interest or relevance - such as vacation jobs or projects, so be prepared to have your answers ready about everything you have put on your application.

Interviewers often expect interviewees to talk much more than the candidates themselves expect to. So don't be too brief in your answers but don't rabbit on for too long either. Watch how the interviewer is reacting to the length of your answers and pause from time to time. S/he will either encourage you to continue or will introduce another question. It is ok to pause and take a breath if you need to give a question a little thought before you answer. You're not expected to speed gabble your way through the interview. A short gap to gather yourself shows thoughtfulness, assertiveness and self-confidence.

Lastly, be polite, but don't be afraid to enter into a discussion and stand your ground if you feel that the interviewers are leading you somewhere you do not agree with or feel to be wrong. This is often an interviewing strategy that is used to see how assertive interviewees are about standing up for their values or beliefs even when put under pressure. Some interviewers will deliberately challenge your replies in order to stimulate this kind of discussion.

## Telephone interviews

It is not unusual to be offered a telephone interview before the company makes a decision on who to short-list for a face-to-face interview, particularly if there are several candidates of a similar level. You must treat a telephone interview with the same formality and importance as a face-to-face interview. Many candidates can fall into the trap of being too informal, because they are having a chat from their own home. So do the same preparation as if you have been called to the interview venue, and be ready to convey 100% professionalism. Here are some tips that will give you the best chance of making it through to the next round:

- Phones are complicated these days. Make sure that yours doesn't 'beep' when you are on a call to alert you to a text message.
- Be absolutely sure not to have 'call waiting' set up on your phone. Nothing is more important right now than you and this telephone interview.
- Seal off a quiet room for yourself that is free of children, pets, or a partner who is stressing in the kitchen, don't be like me that had a baby sitting next to me while taking a telephone interview, of course I flopped it because I was a bit distracted, now before you cast that stone, I had no clue a telephone interview was part of the interview process for the role I applied for, that's why you need to ask ahead of time.
- Have all your documents to hand in a portfolio, in logical order so that you can easily find a necessary document.
- Keep a drink close to hand too; having a dry mouth can be inevitable when the pressure mounts during an interview.
- Don't take the call in your pyjamas. The interviewers can't see you, but you can. You will feel more suited to the occasion if you dress for it.
- Use the phone in its traditional' earpiece' 'mouthpiece' mode – speakerphone can affect your ability to focus.
- Sound enthusiastic and upbeat (but not deliriously so!) You need to come across as a positive, engaging person.
- Enunciate your words clearly, and don't rush; take your time in saying what you need to say.
- Have key documents to hand and offer to scan them, email them as attachments, or post them as hard copies as soon as you have finished the call.
- When you finish speaking with the interviewer, express your interest in the role and ask how your application proceeds from here.

- Thank the interviewer for their time, and do ask them for their contact details so that you can send a note of appreciation for their time (you don't have to, if you don't want).

## Special focus: tips for academic interviews

Academic interviews focus on similar preparation pointers to the ones we have discussed for jobs in other sectors. However, there is much more in-depth preparation to be done. You will need to rigorously research the interviewers, the institution itself (since they all have a different ethos), and every detail about the post on offer. Academia can have a confusing array of different contracts – temporary, permanent, full-time, part-time, occasional, and so on.

Here are some tips to ensure that you are prepared to the highest standard:

- Find out who your interviewers are, and check thoroughly on their academic background. Be aware of their major publications, any honorary residency positions they have held at prestigious universities, and what their current academic research interests are.
- Research the institution. Every university has a good reputation for a particular field of research or scholarship. Be sure to be well aware of what this is, and be able to discuss it at a fairly general level, even if just for small-talk before or after the interview. But some interviewers will want to know why an academic is applying for a job with their particular institution.
- Universities often recruit for several departments at the same time, to fill several different roles – part-time, full-time, senior lecturer, occasional lecturer, undergraduate tutor? Make sure you've read the specification for the role you are applying for. There might also be the opportunity to negotiate on your contract hours if they are particularly impressed with your interview.
- Travelling to the interview: some candidates who come from overseas have their expenses paid, so keep all receipts. If you live within the area, plan your route– Universities are served

by busy bus routes and can be difficult to reach at peak hours, especially if you have to find parking. And it can take 15 – 30 minutes to find your way around the campus to where you need to be. It is advisable to give yourself 1 ½ hours extra time, then have a coffee on campus.

- As you can see from the academic CV/Resume template I provided in Chapter 2, it is a long, involved piece that requires a lot of information. You could be asked about anything, from any point in your academic career. You might not remember that conference paper you delivered in Budapest in 2006 or a paper that you had published in 2004.

- Figure out if the university is primarily about research or teaching, and tailor your experience accordingly. If you have an equal balance of teaching and research experience, sell them both but weight them towards one direction over the other – whatever is most appropriate.

- Be able to explain your past career choices, how they progressed to your present academic endeavours, and how you plan your future academic career aspirations.

- Again, Match! Match!! Match!!! Put your attributes together with the job description, and describe your skills and experience in exactly the terms they are looking for. Remember that by the time they shortlist you for interview, they want you to be the person they are looking for; all you have to do is give the answers that will confirm this for them!

- Academia is all about networking, and everyone knows someone from a conference, previous Ph.D. supervision, or a collaborative piece of research. So don't be shy about letting people know that you have been offered this interview; someone you speak with may know a member of the interview panel, or may have contacts within the department to which you are applying.

## Types of interview questions and how to handle them

Regardless of what kind of job or interview you have been shortlisted for, each type has several general questions that you could be asked for any role, from graphic designer to emeritus professor, it took me series and series of interviews and capacity training to get a grip on some of these questions and their respective answers, so count yourself privileged that now you have it up your sleeves.

Here are some typical questions you can expect to be asked at interviews. These examples include questions about yourself, your professional background (and life experience if you feel it appropriate to share), and your future ambitions.

- **Tell me about yourself:** this can be bewildering if you haven't planned it out, during one of the capacity building training myself and my team conducted few months ago, I asked one of the students this particular question, and he went about telling me his family history how he is the first born out of five children, how he grew up in Nigeria bla bla bla, trust me, your interviewers don't want to know jack about your family history all they want to know are the qualities, skills and experience you've got and how it will be useful to them.

Now most people generally freeze when asked to describe themselves – after all, how do you summarize a whole personality lived in a whole lifetime? The trick is not to attempt to do this. Plan out beforehand what you feel are the most important and relevant things about yourself that will impress the interviewers.

*Sample answer: "Well, when I look back at my track history of employment experience, I feel that it is by sheer determination that I am attending this interview now. Professionally, one of my gifts is to have no fear about leaving a particular sector if an opportunity comes up in a different industry. If I feel I need to go through all of the intellectual reasoning and I still feel sure in my heart that I would love this job, I go for it. I have never been wrong, and the variety of experience and skills I have gained along the way have opened up so many more doors of opportunity for me.*

**Here are some more examples:**

*"my first proper job was 'x'; I worked in that for two years, then I saw a job come up in the arts and media sector, as PA to a highly reputable*

*photographer. I decided that I wanted to stay working in the arts but to move away from the glamour of front line photography. So when I saw an advert for an 'arts for people with disabilities' project, I applied to be project manager and got the job. My patience, tolerance and communication skills all developed, plus I was able to be completely autonomous in my work, and I enjoyed the responsibility that came with it to do things the right way. I am now meticulous about working to the highest standard in any job – no-one can be perfect all the time, or even some of the time. But by nevertheless striving for perfection, I find that I can produce work as close as possible to the highest standard required by my employer.*

**Why did you choose the university you chose/ your degree subject?** The answer to this needs to show ambition and initiative. Answers such as 'my friends were going there' or 'that city has some great bars' are off the map! Explain how you developed your interest in the subject and researched universities to find the most up to date teaching modules on it.

*"To give you the context, I don't mind sharing with you that things were tough at home when I was growing up. I studied an apprenticeship in carpentry first so that I could have a trade and earn a salary from that. I built up a reputation so I was able to pick and choose between jobs. Once I was in this position, I went to university to study what really fascinated me – criminology and psychology. I visited several universities in different parts of the country and researched which ones had the highest reputation for teaching these subjects. I didn't care where I had to move to, I just needed access to the best course.*

- **Explain gaps on your application form** – career break, unemployment, travel, etc.: sometimes life throws some whopping unexpected curveballs our way. Unemployment is a very real part of today's economy so don't feel that it is something you have to hide. Explain whether you were made redundant or fired from a job; if the latter, think of the strengths and positives you gained from the experience.
  *We have already discussed gaps on your application form in fuller detail above, because it can be a worrying issue for people so it deserved to have more space for discussion.*

- **How would the experiences you describe be useful in this company?** Interviewers have several different ways of asking you why you're the right person for the job. Remember that job seeking is all about selling yourself, so plan out well in advance how your previous experiences match the requirements of the job you are currently applying for.

  *"Well for starters, I had to be the bread-winner at home from a young age, and take responsibility for my younger siblings. I studied sociology at university and was seconded on placements to different support sectors across society. I saw limitations in how the local authorities were dealing with issues such as homelessness, family poverty and child neglect. My experiences 'on the ground' as it were, as well as my academic insight into the subject of social issues spurred me to enter the local authority as a housing officer. I could see how promotion opportunities were rolled out through commitment to the job, personal attributes such as sincerity, compassion, etc. I worked my way up to senior housing officer, and then to senior manager of the housing support team. Our work was intense and I had to be constantly on my toes as manager, because the team depended on my being able to make quick, clear-sighted decisions if they were unable to deal with a problem. I learned so much as a senior manager about being organized, having professional boundaries but also being approachable to my team-members. Strategically I developed the communication skills to meet with stake-holders, care quality regulators, and my own senior managers. So it is no wonder that I am sitting here today pursuing a senior management position with you!"*

- **What are your main strengths?:** You'll probably find it difficult to think of these by yourself. Ask yourself what your friends or family say about you – positive and negative. Better still, bring them over for lunch and ask them yourself. You'll be amazed at how different you come across to other people to the person you perceive yourself to be.

  *"One of my main strengths is communication. From having worked as a front desk receptionist in my early career to chair board meetings*

*with my current company, my communication skills have progressed with me as I moved up through the ranks. I am commended on being 'personable and warmly professional' by many people I have worked with or met professionally."*

## What are your weaknesses?

If the interviewer asks about your strengths, they will almost certainly ask about your weaknesses too. Being unable to describe any weaknesses suggests to the interviewer that you lack self-awareness or are a bit egotistical – are you really saying that you are completely perfect at everything that you do?

Pick a couple of minor weaknesses that are of little relevance to the job. For example, if the job involves a lot of contact with customers and colleagues, then you can say that you get bored when you have to spend a lot of time working on your own. Or if the job offers you a lot of independence and flexibility, you may argue that one of your weaknesses is that you get very frustrated when you are micromanaged. When discussing your weaknesses, always talk about how you compensate for them, too. Describe the actions or steps that you take to ensure that your weaknesses don't affect your performance at work.

### Below is how you can answer this question:

*"My main weakness is that I worry too much, unnecessarily. I learned (to focus on what is positive rather than worrying about the negative which hasn't happened or might not) to dissolve the worries. I have been practicing this for six months now and it has made a real difference to my being able to deal with stressful situations calmly, with a realistic attitude."*

- **What other jobs/careers are you applying for?** Be honest in this – if you have sent out stacks of applications, tell the interviewer about which other sectors/areas you are applying for. If you're applying to a number of different areas you can explain that you have faith in your transferable skills and can adapt to different roles. Do praise the company who has called you for interview – state that you are particularly interested in working for this company and explain why. Tell them also that you would turn down other job offers to take up employment with this one.

*"I have actually only applied for this job. I am already in employment but I have always been aware of the positives of this company – a progressive, no-nonsense approach, excellent client care and staff care, and a real sense within the company that everyone is passionate about what they do. I want to be part of such a positive, dynamic team." Or:*

*"I have actually been out of work since I was made redundant six months ago. It is demoralizing going every week to the job centre or checking the newspapers for job adverts so I devised a strategic plan of the kinds of sectors I would be keen to work in, my necessary salary range, and companies that I already know if, which I can research to see if they fit my values. It keeps me busy – applying for jobs can be a full-time job in itself.*

*If I send off two or three applications in a week I number them 1 – 3 (or to whatever number) in priority of who I would most like to work for. Yours was a clear 'no. 1' (your values align with my own, you have an excellent reputation and an outstanding staff retention rate). I guess I am figuring out the difference between what could turn out to be a stagnant job or a dynamic career, in which I could use my full potential and all of this energy I have saved while being unemployed.*

- **Where do you see yourself in five years› time?:** This is a common question; The truth is that you probably don't know what you want to be doing in five years' time – but you can't say that to interviewers as they may take it as a sign of lack of forethought. So read the employer's brochure to get an idea of the normal pace of graduate career development. Be ambitious but realistic. Employers will be impressed to hear that you will not be happy to remain in the same position for the next five years. Answer that you intend to gain as much in-depth knowledge about how the company operates, and would like to work with mentors if there are opportunities, to increase your chances of promotion. In a more senior position you are responsible for leading teams in the correct manner, and you will also have more significant contact with clients.

*"It's funny, but when I was writing the application for this job I was already thinking of where I might be in five years' time. I anticipate that I will spend the first three years really getting to know how everything works within your own company, and how your particular approach fits with the wider picture of the overall industry. I would start to work towards promotion by year three to four, and I would hope to have created a strong, trustworthy reputation by five years. I foresee myself then applying for more senior positions, where I have overall responsibility for staff morale and efficiency, and direct responsibility for the customer's satisfaction.*

- **Tell me about your vacation work, volunteering or involvement with societies, sporting activities, etc.:** if you are a graduate this is where you can really show that you have the requisite skills and experience for the job. Draw on every aspect of work experience that you believe is relevant and discuss it with the interviewers, making the links very obvious without going over the top.

*"My two greatest passions are motor-biking and sailing. Motor-biking is a solo effort and requires complete concentration, but the reward is the thrill of the risk-taking aspect. Sailing is completely different – it involves complete teamwork, down to the tightest schedule. Everyone needs to know where they should be and what they should be doing, but it's as much an*

*opportunity to socialize together while being rejuvenated by the calm of the ocean.*

*I have always found that as long as I can continue these two passions of mine wherever I move to, I don't mind having to relocate for work. I am grounded within myself but these interests give the mind a different perspective about where to live, what keeps us there, and when it's worth taking a risk and moving on. This has led to me finding employment in Dubai for ten years, then coming home and living with my wife and son, close to where my parents live in a small local community. I can take either situation, and one of the biggest deciding factors is where I can find the right job.*

**Questions about your knowledge of the employer, or career area** This is where you draw on your research to show the interviewer that you have taken enough interest in the company to attend your interview knowing as much as possible about it:

- **Why do you want to work for us?** We have looked in detail at this answer above, with a sample answer. Again, just spell out the positives of the company in terms of values, staff support, opportunities for promotion, client satisfaction, and why you think this is the best company to work for in your chosen career area.

- **Why have you chosen to apply for this job?** This is about why you have chosen a particular role in your area of interest. It is an opportunity to state your strengths again as you explain why you are more suited to this particular job function as compared with others in the same sector. In fact, use this opportunity to use keywords that match you with the specific job role, to hammer home the message that who they are looking for is seated right in front of them.

  *"I have had an **entrepreneurial spirit** ever since I sold my sister's toys from a wheelbarrow at our local market when I was a child. I made plenty of profit but had to give it all back to her when my parents found out what I'd done!*

I have **excellent communication and negotiation skills,** and my previous jobs have all given me the opportunity to either market or sell products, or to sell new ideas and concepts to shareholders who were reluctant to see the company move forward.

I am **motivated by success;** my motto has always been that if I strive for the best outcome for the company I work for, my success will reward me with the opportunity to progress.

I have always been commended on being an **excellent team leader;** I am **fair, supportive, and good at problem-solving** so if something goes wrong we can **work towards a solution** together. I believe in fixing situations, not blaming people. However, I can also be very firm if someone is not taking the full responsibility of their role.

- **Who do you think are, or will be, our main competitors?** You will have researched this. Name one or two main competitors and explain why you feel that they compete strongly with the company who are interviewing you. Also explain how the weaknesses that cause them to fall behind the company, and how those weaknesses put you off applying for the same job with competitors.

  *"I want to be an interior designer with your firm because artistically, I feel that you are far beyond the level of your two other competitors in this town. I want to exercise my creativity to bring a little bit of originality to people's homes, depending on their taste. Your two competitors have very standard, dated styles.*

  *The problem I would foresee however is that because this is a relatively small town, people tend to shop where they have built up their loyalties over time, rather than going to where the quality and new ideas are."*

- **What do you think makes you suitable for this job?** This is yet another way of asking 'why do you think you are the right person for this job?' They won't ask you every one of these versions of the question but it is worth your while having as many versions as possible prepared so that you are not caught out on the day. There are multitudes of reasons why you are suitable for the job, so make sure to use every opportunity to get them all in, without it appearing that you are repeating yourself.

*"I have described my best attributes in detail in response to other questions that you have asked me already. Let me summarize them: 1) I have followed your company for a long time, and it has been my ambition to work for you, because I feel that I will have the best opportunity here to put my skills to good use.*

*In terms of values we seem to read from the same page, so I don't foresee that there will be any conflict between what I believe to be right against what you believe to be right. Ultimately anyway, the company decides what is right, but because I share your values and concepts, I will willingly work with your instruction, without the resentment of an employee who doesn't share your values.*

*Also, because I have followed your company for such a long time, I will be a natural representative for you, because I will be entirely comfortable in outlining the attributes of your company and the opportunities that you can extend to new clients, new share-holders or even new staff.*

*I have built up extensive team-member experience and senior-management experience throughout my career so I could fit into either role and be comfortable with it.*

*In the past I was in charge of PR and media management for a medium to large sized business. I can market or advertise you originally and entirely faithful to what you do and what you promise.*

- **What do you see as the main threats or opportunities facing the company?** To answer this question, think about political, economic, social and technological contexts. They may not be affected by all four of these factors but they serve as a useful framework to really dig deep into how a company operates and is likely to be operating in five years' time.

*"This company once had a reputation for making the best car models in the world. Now your value is less recognized by the government, who is providing no financial help to support your existence as a 'national treasure' of the manufacturing industry. Economically, not many people are buying new cars these days, but the wealthy elite are not affected by the global financial crisis, so you always have a potential customer base there. Socially, if you start to offer ordinary working people the opportunity to buy your cars and pay for them interest-free over five years, you run the risk of defaulted payments as more people are made redundant. On the other hand though, by offering this very deal to new customers at least you are preserving your business and keeping car production running. People always feel good about themselves when they buy a new car – that is the social mood that you can tap into, which could offer a strong potential for survival and profit until whenever this recession ends.*

*Another opportunity is that there have never been so many technological experts out of work, and car manufacturing is hugely reliant on technology design and maintenance today. You can set your own price for technology staff salary and offer opportunities for promotion up through the ranks. Your company could actually become one of the local hubs of employment.*

- **What image do you have of this company?** If you offer an image of the company of a Victorian workhouse mistreating its employees and keeping them on the poverty line, you shouldn't be attending that interview in the first place! When you talk about the 'image' of the company talk about clever but sophisticated marketing and branding content and images. If the company has a long respected history, talk about it has a progressive, contemporary image without losing any of its renown for having been in the business for a long time. See what aspects of the company appealed to you, and decide how you can tie these in to your assessment of the company's image. There is something about how the company looks, feels and operates that has drawn you there.

*"I first had contact with your recruitment centre when I was out of work and went to look at job prospects. The atmosphere there was fun and relaxed, but sharply professional. Your staff listened to me and made everything I explained to them relevant to my application. They phoned me with daily updates on recruiters who were interested with me. They advised me on a base salary that I was worth through my experience and put me forward for jobs of this salary or higher.*

*This was one of the best, most professional customer service experiences I have ever had, and now that I have gained some experience in the recruitment business with another company when I was living in Canada, I want to work with your team. The company as a whole appears sharp and contemporary, but warm and inviting. That is the kind of environment I want to work in.*

## MANAGING CLOSED QUESTIONS

These are questions which can normally be answered with a simple "yes" or "no". They are difficult because they don't give you the opportunity to expand on the context of your answers. This is actually a way of putting you under pressure to sell yourself. Recruiters now seem to put great weight on the ability to "sell" the skills gained in your work experience. If you are asked a closed question open it up, as in the following example:

***Interviewer: "Did you enjoy your customer care training course?"***

The simple answer to this would be to reply 'yes' or 'no'. The way the question is put can trick you into leaving it at that. But 'yes' or 'no' is not going to be of interest to the interviewer unless you expand on why the course has been of value to you.

***Interviewee 1: "Yes."***
***Interviewee 2: "Yes, I've found it a very interesting course because ..."***

Many candidates feel that their casual shop or restaurant job is of no interest to employers, but nothing could be further from the truth. Recruiters expect you to be able to explain the skills you gained serving customers, working in a busy team, being tactful when handling complaints, and so on. This can include voluntary work but preferably anything that demonstrates leadership skills, ability to work as part of a team, and customer service experience (retail, hospitality, call centers – anything that involves putting the customer first). Being aware of the competencies you have developed through casual work impresses employers, because it shows that you can learn lessons and strengths from even what you might consider to be menial work.

## ARRIVING FOR THE INTERVIEW

So you've done your research, prepared inside-out for how to answer questions about yourself, and now the big day is here. To go in there and make the best impression, the show is only starting. Here are the most important guidelines that you need to remember to get through it successfully.

- **Try to arrive ten or fifteen minutes early**: This doesn't only give you the opportunity to visit the loo – time spent waiting in the reception area can be very useful if there are publications about the employer or their field of work to read. There are usually some copies of the company's annual review to read in the reception waiting area. Arriving early enough also helps you get used to the atmosphere of the company environment so that you feel somewhat orientated by the time you enter the interview room. Be friendly and polite to everyone you meet, including receptionists, porters and security staff.

- **Dress smartly but comfortably.** If you look good, you will feel good. Men are advised to wear a matching two piece suit with a plain shirt and sensible tie. Grey, navy and black are all suitable. Females are advised to dress smartly without being too fashionable (unless you are applying for a job in the fashion industry or something related), and definitely do not dress too sexily. Go for more neutral or dark shades –nothing that screams bright or loud. Keep your make-up fairly subtle; a 'daytime' look rather than a 'night out' look.

- **Start the interview in a positive manner and it** is likely to continue in this vein. Smile, and make eye contact. A firm handshake at the start will help a lot too.

## FIRST IMPRESSIONS

Your appearance, your manner, your handshake -- these are all very important and they set the tone for the rest of the interview. According to a survey of 1000 recruiters by Fly Research three quarters of interviews are lost within three minutes of entering the room. Research by Springbett found that 85% of interviews were decided in the first two to three minutes. Here are some surprising facts:

- 25% of interviewers were put off by **a weak handshake** or **lack of eye contact**
- 24% were put off by **poor body language**
- 18% put off by **poor posture** (e.g. slumped shoulders suggests lack of energy or lack of confidence) and a reluctant presence

All the research suggests that selectors make snap judgments about your trustworthiness, attractiveness, competitiveness and aggressiveness, and spend the rest of the interview confirming or denying these opinions.

Only 20% waited until the middle of the interview to test a candidate on their knowledge of the industry and aptitude for the job. Their mind was already made up by the 'silent' factors outlined above.

So how do you make that all-important good impression at the start of an interview?

- **Shake hands firmly and warmly**, but wait to be invited to sit down. Handshakes are also commonly given at the end of the interview. Here's a bit of interesting trivia – handshakes originated as a way for knights to show that they didn't have concealed weapons. A firm handshake is perceived to communicate sociability, friendliness and assertiveness, all desirable qualities in candidates, whereas weak handshakes may communicate introversion, shyness and even neuroticism, signaled by the lack of engagement that the handshake communicates. Also, as the handshake is made at the start of the interview it can set a positive tone for the rest of the encounter. In practice interviews with 98 students, those who gave a firm handshake were more likely to be offered jobs. Women who gave a firm handshake were perceived more positively than men who gave a firm handshake.

- **Smile** at the interviewer: *"Smiling appears to be a central ingredient in successfully interviewing for a job."* This is the finding of a study which explains that a smiling candidate was rated as more attractive than the same person with a neutral expression. This was only true when the smiling person was looking at the other person; when she was smiling but looking sideways, the neutral expression was rated more favourably. So to attract someone (and I mean in terms of winning them over with your personality) – smile and look at them, and don't forget to use eye contact to engage them.

- **Eye contact:** It is impossible to converse with someone properly without making some eye contact with the person. It shows them that you don't trust them enough to fully engage with them, and it shows you how unconfident you are about what you are saying. Failure to make adequate eye contact gives an impression of nervousness and lack of self-esteem. Unfortunately it can come across to others as being dishonest and untruthful. In an interview you don't want to be misunderstood and perceived as being aloof, unnecessarily anxious or a dishonest. The balancing line of this is not to outstare your interviewers either. That can send the wrong signal, that you are being aggressive and challenging.

- **You may be offered tea or coffee.** If you feel this will help you to relax, then fine, but otherwise it is OK to refuse politely. If caffeine makes you anxious, definitely refuse politely.

- **Be aware of your body language throughout the interview:** So you've entered the interview room with positivity, good eye contact, a firm handshake and an engaging smile. What you absolutely don't want is to undo this spectacular entrance by forgetting about your body language later – it is guaranteed to do more talking than you do! Don't make yourself stiff and uncomfortable, just be aware of your posture and make sure not to slouch, or laze back halfway down the chair. Sit upright but in a natural position, try to remember not to cross your arms. If you tend to fidget a lot with your hands, the hardest thing in the world is not doing so. It's your call on this – if your hands feel awkward and impossible to appear relaxed, you can fidget discreetly by wearing a ring on your finger and turning it with the other hand. Don't tap your legs, the desk in front of you, the side of your chair, or anywhere else!

- **Speak clearly and not too fast.** Remember to pause and think to avoid blathering rubbish.

- **Don't use fidget words:** Is there a meaning to this question? Actually yes. In normal every-day speech we all use meaningless 'filler' expressions … 'like', 'you know?', 'you get me so far?' 'I mean', and so on. Try to rehearse your answers and the things you want to say before the interview so you can be fluent in your speech in the actual event.

**Special Focus: some cringe-worthy interview answers**

- An interviewee is asked a question he knows nothing about, so he decides to try and bluff it. Full of 'er', 'um', 'you get me?' and so on, he tried to come up with an answer but crashes. So he tries again to word this "answer" in a different way, and crashes twice. He bursts into tears at the end of the interview as the interview panel thanks him for his time and tells him that they'll be in touch when they decide on a candidate.

- A female interviewee was asked a question related to protecting victims of domestic abuse when she went for a health and social care job. The answer she gave was the direct opposite of the best practice standards that every health and social care employee is required to uphold by law. The interviewers quickly brought the interview to a close and informed her straightaway that she would not be offered the job.
  She also left in tears.

- A female interviewee was asked about her hobbies and interests, so she listed things like tennis, cooking and driving. The interview panel asked her what she most loves to spend her free time doing. She explained that she'd had a strict Christian upbringing and had only recently become *sexually liberated, so "having sex – loads of it"* was her answer.

- The interviewers put the interviewee on the spot: *"as you know, this job is Child Protection, and most of your work history has been working with vulnerable adults. Do you think that you will enjoy working with children?"* The interviewee answered *"I honestly haven't a clue."*

- An interviewee applying for a job with asylum seekers was asked about her best qualities. Her reply was "Pretty much everything I've gone on about so far. Yeah, they're my qualities. Hm." Puzzled faces around the interview panel table.

- A very tall male interviewee trips on the runner that crosses the doorway into the interview room and literally flies into the room, then lands flat on his face. The interviewers are startled, and it takes the interviewee about 15 minutes to recover from his shock.

- An interviewee turns up dressed casually for a group interview with psychometric testing. She walks into the room and everyone, male and female, are wearing suits. The men are very formal, also wearing ties. She is the only person in the room wearing kitten heels and ripped jeans.
- An interviewee put on his application that he loves all kinds of music. One of the interviewers asked him *"So what would you do if we asked you to rap the answers to the next three questions?"* He wasn't listening properly because his anxiety was distracting him, so he thought that the interview panel actually had asked him to rap the next three answers. And he did.

## A LITTLE RESEARCH INTO THE X FACTOR THAT CLINCHES THE JOB

The standard method of selecting candidates for jobs is to make list of key competencies required in the job and then to match these to the candidate's application. However two US researchers (Higgins & Judge) followed 100 university students trying to get their first job. They analyzed their CV/Resumes/Resumes for qualifications and work experience and talked to the interviewers afterwards. Surprisingly, the main factor for the interviewers in deciding which ones were selected was whether or not the candidate appeared to be a pleasant individual. The successful candidates:

- Smiled and made a lot of eye contact.
- Showed a genuine interest in the interviewer and gave genuine compliments (in a professional context, not about hair, suits or outfits!)
- Praised the company
- – we've touched on this already, but it's important to find something you genuinely like about the organisation.
  Asked interesting questions

- There is no problem with asking one of the interviewers something like "What is your personal experience of working for this company?"
- Talked about subjects unrelated to the job, but that interested the candidate and interviewer. Try to be well read before the interview and have a wider range of conversation beyond the three main points – you, the job and the organisation.

## THE PANIC FACTOR: HOW TO OVERCOME INTERVIEW FEARS

You might be wondering at this stage how anyone gets through an interview. It feels like trying to pat your head, rub your tummy and move your foot round in circles all at the same time! Try to relax, interviews have been used since the early 20th Century to select candidates for jobs. Here are some tips to give you a wider sense of perspective on the interviewing process that should help keep your anxiety under control:

- **Try to believe that it's not so important:** I know in the current economy, job interviews are precious. But if you don't get this one, don't worry. Look on it as valuable experience and request feedback from the HR department. There will be other interviews in future and it's not the end of the world if you don't get this job. Keeping this mind-set helps you build your confidence and focus on the actual interview itself rather than on how badly you need the job, which creates nervousness and desperation.
- **Preparation is key:** the more preparation you have done, such as working out answers to common interview questions and doing careful research on the organisation and job, the more likely you are to be successful. You will go into the interview room confident of being ready to answer most questions that come your way and relaxed enough to deal with those unexpected curveballs.

- **Try out some visualization:** even if you haven't done it before. If you are skeptical about using mental exercises to deal with anxiety, put your skepticism to one side for the moment and try to believe that visualization will work for you. It's simple, the night before the interview, visualize yourself undergoing the whole process, step by step, and imagine everything going really well. You are answering questions fluently and with confidence, and you can feel that there is a positive chemistry between you and the interviewers. They like you, they are impressed with what you have to say. Ultimately, you get the job.

- **Don't worry too much about making a mistake:** nearly everyone fluffs one question and a lot of research into recruitment finds that interviewers prefer candidates who come across as being human ("To err is human, to forgive divine.") to those who appear "plastic perfect". Professor Sian Bellock investigated why our performance reduces under pressure and suggested that *"getting people to write about their worries beforehand ... can really help ... Writing about your worries almost "downloads" them so they are less likely to pop up and impact your performance."* So the day before your interview, spend some time writing down everything that you are worried about. And when you have finished, give yourself some leeway to answer at least one question a bit clumsily.

- **Practise! Practise!! Practise!!!** So you've done all your research and preparation, and written down all your worries. Now it's time to do some verbal practice so that the words come to you automatically. Hand over your research and preparation questions to someone who will practise with you and keep it serious. The last thing you want to do is fall about laughing, because you'll associate that with giving the same answer in the actual interview. Go over the questions until you feel that you can answer them comfortably.

- **Bring a notepad and pen:** you can take notes during the interview as long as you jot down the information during a brief pause in the conversation.

- **Know in advance what format the interview will take:** your invitation to attend the interview should give you all the details you need to know about it, but there's no time lost in phoning up HR to make sure that no details have been missed out on the letter.

- **Plan your route:** you wouldn't believe how many people think 'oh that's only a 45 minute drive' and leave exactly 45 minutes before the interview. It doesn't matter if you know the journey by the back of your hand or not – plan your route, plan an alternative route in case you run into any disaster that's likely to happen on the road that day, and leave in plenty of time to make a detour if you need to, and still arrive early.

- Lastly, **be honest with yourself about your interest in the job** – many CV/Resumes by perfectly qualified people are turned down because they are not passionate enough about the job.

## Special focus A: five minute calming techniques

Your first weapon is the knowledge that changing the rate and regularity of your breath can change how you feel. The breath controls the heart rate, which in turn controls the thoughts your brain produces. When you're in an anxious state your breath becomes fast, shallow and erratic, your heart beats quickly, and as a result, your brain produces anxious thoughts which turn the whole process into a vicious circle.

So the key is to slow down and regulate the rhythm of your breathing:

- Find a quiet place where you will be undisturbed for at least five minutes. You can do this with your eyes open, so it's fine to do on a taxi or in a public place as long as no-one tries to speak to you.

- With your palm flat on your stomach, breathe in and draw your breath all the way down to meet your hand. This expands the volume of oxygen you take into your lungs.
  * Hold for a slow count of five.
  * Exhale for another count of five.
  * Hold this exhalation and count slowly to two.

- Repeat the whole exercise until five minutes are up. You could set a timer on your mobile phone so that you can relax into it and don't have to worry about watching the time.
- Here's where the visualization comes in. As you inhale, imagine clear, minty-blue fresh bright air entering your lungs and expanding through your whole body. As you exhale, imagine that your breath is smoky and discoloured – this is your anxiety being released from the body.
- Visualize all of the parts of your body that are being affected by your anxiety – a knot in your stomach, sweaty palms, tension in your muscles, and imagine all of these symptoms being released with your exhalations. Visualize yourself feeling more confident, and your thoughts are collected and ready to turn into winning answers in the interview.
- When you are ready to come back to consciousness again sit up slowly and take a few minutes to come fully awake again.

**Special focus B: A word on make-up and grooming for female interview candidates**

Women have always had a hard time dressing and grooming to please others. For all that the feminist movements throughout the 20th and 21st Century have achieved, women are still judged – often unconsciously – on the attention they pay to their make-up and general appearance. But where do you draw an acceptable line between toning it down if you are a 'love makeup' person or winding it up if you are a 'natural no makeup' person? Unfortunately, employers do score for making a visible effort with your appearance and grooming. Fortunately, there are some tips and guidelines to get the look just right.

- Nail varnish must be perfect, or wear none at all. Chipped nail varnish either seems unprepared or it suggests that you have been biting your nails in terror in reception. Also, it's one of the first things people notice when they shake hands with you.
- Hair doesn't get off the hook either. It should be freshly washed, not too laden with products, especially highly scented ones. If you have long hair, style it elegantly so that it doesn't hang

in your face during the interview. Split ends are apparently annoying to recruiters too – they are connected with laziness and not being concerned about your appearance.

- The majority of recruiters who were surveyed by Debenhams on how they feel about make-up said that they prefer that mascara is worn, but it should be freshly applied. Stale or smudged mascara can give the impression that you have attended the interview in last night's makeup.

- On the other hand, don't overkill either. No heavily penciled eyebrows for example. As much as we might love movies based on the 1920s era, recruiters want to see you use stylish, contemporary makeup techniques.

- Don't wear too much perfume or an overpowering scent – the interviewer will smell you rather than pay attention to you, and want that scent gone from the room as quickly as possible!

- Lipstick can warm your face and bring colour to it. Wear a subtle shade of lipstick that suits your skin tone. No bright red or pink.

- Clothing should be smart. Women are generally advised to dress smartly in either a skirt-suit or a trouser-suit. The same as for men, wear a shirt (or blouse) of a fairly neutral colour. If it has any, the print should be subtle and muted; absolutely no large patterns or loud colours.

- Footwear: if you like to wear heels, keep them to no more than 3". The interviewers will be looking for a measure of common sense in how you dress, and stilettos can be a symbol of outrageousness in a formal situation such as this.

I know this seems like a stringent set of guidelines to follow, but after doing all that research and preparation it is best to start off on the right foot (with the right shoes!) and make the right impression with your appearance. You will gain extra confident from knowing that your appearance fits the part, so you can relax and focus on the questions. In Chapter 4 we are going to look in detail at the most common categories of interview questions.

# CHAPTER 4:

# THE MOST COMMON INTERVIEW CATEGORIES OF QUESTIONS

In this chapter we are going to look at interview questions – lots and lots of them! They are all grouped into some main categories so once you become accustomed to them they become easier to remember. Together, these different themes form a well-rounded test of who you are as an individual and how you come across as a professional.

- About you (experience, attributes and qualities, life experience)
- About your professional experience
- Why you want the job
- Why you think you are suitable for this job
- Questions about your employment history, education, volunteering work
- Curveball questions – favourite colour, what luxury item would you have on a desert island, etc. These questions are asked to put you under pressure and see how well you can think on your feet/ improvise in a pressured situation.

## RECOGNIZING WHAT INTERVIEWERS ARE LOOKING FOR

At first examination, different job adverts seem to be looking for an astounding range of skills, experience, and qualities, not to mention the confidence to articulate these in an interview. But in actuality, most employers are looking for three key factors for finding the right person for the job. These can be summarized as the three Cs of interviews:

- **Competence:** Interviewers are usually looking to recruit people who have the skills and personal qualities to do the job with minimal or no supervision. You need to be very sure you possess such skill. Of course you will need help and support to learn the ropes when you begin any new job and the employer should make allowances for this in your schedule. Once you know what you're doing and are ready to steam ahead however, your employer will value you for your competence and initiative. (If, on the other hand, you find yourself working with an employer who checks and controls your work in minute detail and won't let you use your competence and initiative, you need to assess whether or not they really value you. If they don't, it's time to look for another job. It won't do your health or home life any good to stay working in a job that suppresses your skills and expertise.)

- **Commitment:** Interviewers always want to give the job to someone who they believe will see it through for at least more than two years. They want a self-motivated person who persists in the face of difficulties and finds ways to solve those problems, rather than giving up at the first sign of trouble. Many people do feel intimidated when things are not running smoothly, and shatter in the face of challenges, or even resign from their job.

- **Chemistry:** Interviewers want someone who they believe they can get along with. The sense of comradeship in a work team is essential to everyone's productivity, and the overall performance of the company. All employers feel they have a unique working culture and therefore want to know that potential employees can fit in with the rest of the team. They want to keep everyone happy and working to their full potential.

# HOW TO MAKE SURE YOU PUT THE 3C ESSENTIALS ACROSS: A WORD ON ARTICULATION

### Using intonation and inflection

Interviewers can spend a couple of days at a time interviewing more personalities than you could believe exist in the world. The irony of it is that they have to ask the same questions over and over, which can get pretty tedious. So the more individual (without being over the top) the candidate is, the more the interviewers are likely to warm up to. They can feel really bored when all candidates seem to be saying pretty much the same thing. One way to make the interviewers sit up and take notice of what you're saying is to pay attention to the focus on your tone of voice. Here are some guidelines on how to articulate yourself with the right balance of calm but also interested and enthusiastic:

- **Introduce inflection into your speech:** Actors sometimes talk of using 'light and shade' in a voice. Occasionally raise the tone of your voice or speed up the pace to convey excitement or passion about a topic. Deepen your voice or slow down a little to transmit seriousness. Make sure that your facial expressions match what you are saying. If you are talking about some intense experiences you have had that give you the edge on other people, don't look bored while you are describing them.

- **Emphasize key words:** Say key words and phrases a little louder to make them stand out. This tactic is the auditory equivalent of typing important words in a **bold** typeface.

- **Articulate your words clearly and carefully:** If you are in any doubt as to whether you pronounce your words properly and clearly, ask a variety of professionals for their opinion. Don't ask friends, as they are too used to your way of speaking to give you objective feedback.

- **Think about leaving pauses between sentences:** remember that full stops appear at the end of sentences, so your speech should run to the same pace and rhythm as how you read punctuation.

- **Don't let your sentences all run togethe**r in the same tone of voice. Intonation and inflection are difficult to get right.
- It can be really annoying to hear someone overdoing it by ending every sentence like a question?
- Like that? Huh? You get me?

  Anyone who grew up with the Friends generation in the 90s is vulnerable to falling prey to this!

  The best way to tell if you sound okay is to tape record yourself practising interview answers out loud and listening to how they come across. Have someone else listen to it too so that you don't over-criticize yourself (many of us cringe at the sound of our own voices on a tape recording!).

## Case study: when the 3Cs go wrong

*"Belle (short for Belinda) had a front line job in the health sector with the civil service and decided to apply for a better one when the opportunity came up. Again, it involved front-line working with the public, and representing statutory healthcare. The organisation she applied to was funded by the civil service but were responsible for their own recruitment and staff management.*

*Unfortunately the hiring managers were not too hot on their 3Cs either, so the first fatal error they made was to interview candidates without paying any attention to the Competence, Commitment and Chemistry trinity. So Belle was hired, and within weeks she was distressing customers by insulting them, and creating enemies within the staff team. Everyone hated working on shift with her.*

*She was given the position of deputy manager because she had excellent clerical skills – if a store cupboard needed to be sorted, or an office desk full of files needed to be organized, she was the one to do it. But she wouldn't think twice about telling a service user that she would report them to the manager if they didn't comply with the organization's rules. Service users started to become afraid of coming to the organisation because if Belle was working that day, she was sure to be aggressive and rude to them.*

*Senior management thought that she had "wonderful assertiveness". Hmmm. As time went on some of the other staff requested to be transferred to other parts of the organisation or back to being managed directly by the civil service. When a normally soft-spoken staff-member challenged her one day, Belle physically manhandled her out of the building and later claimed that the staff-member had pushed a client. More and more complaints were brought to senior management, and the words 'she's a liability, something bad is going to happen if she continues to work in this way' came up practically once a week.*

*The outcome was that Belle <u>did</u> offer commitment and she played this up in every supervision meeting. She raved about how she loved the job and the organisation, how she saw her career future there, and had never had better senior managers. So out of the 3Cs there was no competence, no chemistry, but it was her 'commitment' that won over her superiors.*

Yes, this does happen, so you don't need to grab the first job you are offered if you have misgivings about the company. Ask around, see what kind of experiences other people have had with it. A company with a notorious reputation will be known across the city. Give yourself time to find out what people on the ground are saying about it.

But let's assume that you are being interviewed by the right company. How do you ensure that these three key qualities come across? By answering all your interview questions competently, by engaging pleasantly with the interviewers, and by emphasizing your willingness to make a commitment to the company. Show interest too in what your team is like/who will be your colleagues. And if you can hold your nerve while you feel that all these awkward questions are being thrown at you, you are 99% there in proving to the employer that you can deal with the pressure and be inventive in how you answer the questions. The strongest way that you can create chemistry is to use your tone of voice and body language to demonstrate that you are the kind of likeable person who gets on well with everyone. Be aware that the interviewers are not only evaluating what you say, but also how you say it. No matter what section of the book you turn to, be sure to keep the 'three Cs' in mind.

## HOW MANY INTERVIEWERS WILL THERE BE?

The standard panel of interviewers is two, although depending on the job there might be three, or even four. One-on-one interviews are also common for less demanding jobs. In this situation your interviewer is most likely to be somebody from the personnel department, or in a smaller company they may be from the area of work for which you are applying.

Two-to-one interviews may involve both a personnel and a line manager. This can be trickier for the interviewee as the questions seem to come faster, giving you less time to collect your thoughts between different topics. Also, if they are skilled at interviewing they tend to play 'good cop, bad cop.' Remember to keep your cool, answer as best as you can, and if 'bad cop' is really making you flustered just put your focus on the questions they are asking you, not on the person who is doing the asking.

For senior public and private sector jobs, panel interviews could involve a panel of up to six interviewers. There's no doubt that this is intimidating – it feels like walking onto a stage and being expected to give an impromptu musical performance to an audience. This number of interviewers is relatively rare but if you do find yourself in this situation, just direct your attention to whoever is speaking. When answering questions, begin by directing your answer to the person who asked the question, but as you elaborate try and include the panel as a whole, just by glancing in their direction and making eye contact occasionally. And don't forget the smile!

**Apart from the 'three Cs,' what do recruiters look for?** These skills apply to potential employees at all levels, so as many of these skills you can possess or acquire will ultimately give you an edge over another job seeker. Make notes beside each one and put a cross beside each skill you feel you have not sufficiently developed and see if you can find opportunities to practise a little before the interview.

# COMMUNICATION SKILLS

Since most jobs generally require physical contact with colleagues and customers (you don't have to hug them, but you do share a small physical space with them), it is very important for you to possess good communication skills. So when the interview focuses on your communication skills you need to clearly explain both difficult scenarios and positive ones where your communication skills were valuable to those situations. Give examples of how you expressed your communication skills and how they were to you in your previous job or at school.

**Special focus: more cringe-worthy interview no-no's…**

- Turning up in trainers
- Smelling of last night's beer
- Asking if they do random drug-testing
- Telling them you really need this job because you are poor

**… and more cringe-worthy interview replies**

- Everybody leaves me: you won't want to keep me either
- I heard that the guys who work here are fit … is that true?
- I never stole anything from work, but the petty cash did rest in my account for six months
- What kind of dumb question is that to ask me?
- I left my job because I cannot stand anyone being in charge of me
- I had a dispute with a colleague that we couldn't resolve. The conflict resolution officer intervened to resolve, and now we're both looking for new jobs

- I don't get to use anything more sophisticated than the coffee machine, and even then I get the last lousy cup. So someone lend me their PA to turn on my computer and show me what to do every day?
- I'm a hot-blooded male, oh yeahhhh! (as he loosens his tie)
- My kind of secretary is the one who'll sit on my knee
- I will be ideal for your media and events team, because I network, i.e. party, like the best of 'em
- When asked if the candidate had anything to ask the panel … If you could be a monkey, would you rather live in a jungle or in someone's house?
- I'm going to have a problem getting to work … it's a mile from the train station to the office and my winter coat isn't waterproof
- Can we get through the last bit in the next ten minutes? My friend is giving me a lift home and he's waiting outside. The interviewer asks him *"Well how do you know that he's getting impatient?"* I've my phone on silent in my pocket and he's just buzzed me.
- Do you have 'Moanful Mondays' or interchangeable sick days?
- If I don't get the job I'd love to go out to dinner with you (staring at the interviewer on the left)
- My folks don't really 'get' this job and they wanted me to be a pharmacist. Can you call them and explain how important this job is, and where it can take me?
- So tell me everything about the bonuses, huh?
- Do I have to come in for a drug test on the same day I'm offered the job, if I get it?
- Man, with the price of petrol these days, I need a pay increase – that's why I'm sitting here in front of you guys.
- I want to work for you guys because I have a panic attack every time I go to my current job
- My boss made it clear that he didn't like me – he kept giving me overtime
- My assets, hmmm, my boyfriend told me not to say my double DDs. Oh my God, did I just say that out loud?

**And in response to the question** *"what are your weaknesses?"*...

- Well I once went to an anger management course instead of serving a suspended sentence for aggression ... but you'll have seen all that on my security check by now anyway, won't you? (They wouldn't have, because they only run those checks after they choose a candidate!) I still get angry easily but I remember my 'Don't get Angry ABC' ...
- Not even a bomb wakes me up in good time for work. I always roll out of bed and arrive at work a few minutes late. Is it ok to have my breakfast at my desk?
- I have a problem with drinking and I hope this job brings some stability to my life.
- I've never been good at learning new things or picking things up. I get jealous of people who find it easy because they'll always have a chance at getting a promotion and higher salary. So I'd rather get a job that's normal nine to five and doesn't expect too much of me outside of my routine daily work

**Tell us about your leadership skills**

- I play bridge with my friends and have been the lead player for two years running

**When can you start?**

- Ooh, well I'm still living at home and I've promised to babysit while my parents are away. So can I check with them and get back to you?

**Can you describe yourself in three to five adjectives?**

- Er, does sexy count?
- What's an adjective?
- I don't like to categorize myself, so 'no'!
- Clean, attractive, needy, socially awkward, keen

**And how do you deal with mistakes you have made?**

- I once stole some stationary items from work. I resolved the situation by paying for them after my manager found out and gave me the choice of paying back for them or being fired
- I flap and panic, and try to follow the best possible solution. I always try to keep the mistake under wraps so that no-one else – definitely not my boss – finds out
- In the past I used to always blame the weakest member of my team but I've had therapy since and have learned to take responsibility now
- I usually get a nosebleed and get sent home

**Have you submitted your two weeks' notice to your current employer?**

- Well, no. What I mean is, I've usually left spontaneously without giving any notice, or I've been fired by my manager.

**And some baffling 'almost got the job' replies**

"Are you going to run a criminal check on me?", one candidate asked. Because if you are going to, it might be best for me to have a little chat with you first to give you the background situation of whatever you find." "And what might we find, Mr. Jones?"

**"Whatever", replied Mr. Jones.**

- Several candidates have had no fixed home address because they choose to live in gypsy camps and sites. When they are asked why, their usual response is that they are anti-capitalist and want to rebel against ownership of property and badly divided wealth. "So you are completely against capitalism?"
"Absolutely, it's a filthy concept that has landed the entire planet in a shameful mess."
"Very honourable, I'm sure. But tell us, why are you applying for a job with a global investment bank?"
- One candidate's trousers fell down as he was shaking the interviewers' hands. He was so flustered he felt he had to go

through the polite motions of hand-shaking, and only then did he scrabble down to pull his waistband up.

**Moral of the story: if you are borrowing a suit from a relative, make sure that you are of a similar size!**

- A female candidate tottered into the interview room, and lowered herself into her seat, wincing in pain. Before the interviewers could introduce themselves she said "can we hold for one minute until I take my shoes off? I'm not used to wearing heels and my feet are killing me. You don't mind if I take them off, do you?"
- "You all seem like young and trendy folk, so I can be honest with you. I've got a banging headache from last night … could you call your secretary and ask her to bring in a coffee for me? One sugar, just a drop of milk. Thanks so much."
- "Oh well I'm on community service at the moment. Thank-you so much for inviting me to attend your interview. Could we postpone it until my probation officer says I'm finished and free to have my time back again?"

So these are all the clumsy, some might say "idiotic" answers that can have you struck off the list of possibilities before you can check out your suit in the mirror. But let's have a look at all the ways that you can secure a job or dash your chances of being hired, before you even open your mouth! The next section looks at all aspects of body language that are likely to form a huge part of what you communicate during the interview. You might not realize you are doing some giveaway signs, but the interviewers will be fully honed in on them.

## BODY LANGUAGE

Doing an interview can make you feel split down the middle – paying attention to body language when you enter the room, and trying to give the best possible answers when you are in the interviewee's chair. According to research into nonverbal communication, 55% of our overall communication effectiveness is determined by our body language – the type of gestures we make, what posture we hold, our body movements (such as fidgets, tics or touching our nose every 10 seconds). We all have our characteristic physical presence but try to be aware of cutting out unnecessary gestures and movements throughout the interview. They can be distracting and cause the interviewer to pay less attention to what you are saying.

## Special focus C: Using your body language

They say that actions speak louder than words. You can speak volumes without even opening your mouth. A lot can be said about what is going on inside a person by the way they use their body language. For instance, constantly looking at your wristwatch or tapping your fingers on the table simply implies that you are really not interested in what is going on and you are in a hurry for the whole thing to be over. (Which of course you are! Not many people view an interview as something enjoyable that they want to go on and on. But don't give the impression that you wish it was over.) Repeatedly stroking your hair or looking down is also a sign of nervousness. Below are some tips to help you project yourself properly during an interview:

- **Stand and sit up straight:** Sit at a 90 degrees angle with a straight (but not stiff) long back this lengthens and holds your spine straight, and stops you from slouching. This is the best sitting position to hold because it is relaxed without being too relaxed, and it shows that you are in control of your body, and that you are confident in yourself. Slouching or hunching forward indicates nervousness or exhaustion.

- **Use your hands to emphasize key points:** Hand gestures can make people seem more sincere or credible. So use your hands occasionally to underscore key points and to make yourself visually more engaging. Examples of this are counting points off with your fingers, or turning your palms up and spreading your fingers to indicate sincerity. Only use your hands to emphasize key points when you are speaking. Keep your hands still when the interviewers are speaking to show that you're listening.

Avoid crossing your arms. Some interviewers read crossing of arms as a sign of being defensive or arrogant. However, contrary to popular opinion you may cross your legs – so long as you don't cross your arms across your chest as well. Avoid pointing at the interviewers – this is an aggressive gesture and makes you seem intimidating. Feel like you're patting your head and rubbing your tummy yet? Well there's more ...

- **Keep your legs still:** Get your legs into a comfortable position and then avoid crossing and un-crossing them, or tapping your feet. Such fidgeting can be unnerving and irritating for the interviewers.

- **Smile when you talk about your strengths or achievements:** Smiling would be contradictory when talking about difficult situations at work. But if you are talking about positive aspects of yourself and your working life, do feel comfortable enough to smile occasionally – you come across as being more natural.

- **Smile when you leave the room:** When you say your goodbyes and thank the interviewers for their time, give them another broad smile to show that you enjoyed meeting them, even if you feel that the interview session wasn't a positive experience.

- **Dealing with interview anxiety:** Special Focus A this chapter gives you specific calming techniques that you can do in five minutes. But apart from that, it's important to remind you too to just give yourself a break. Struggling with anxiety is exhausting – it is best to prepare to have to deal with it rather than just worry that it won't go away. It might, it might not, and the chances are that fighting it will make you feel exhausted throughout the interview. You need to feel at your best and most alert to give the strongest answers.

- **Do you have a dry mouth from nervousness?** Accept a glass of water if you are offered one, or ask for it if it is not offered to you. We are all human, we all drink water.

# NEGOTIATION AND PERSUASION

No one likes 'hype' or 'the hard sell', yet a huge part of your job involves keeping customers happy, bringing their investment to new products, and finding new customers. You will also have to convince your colleagues, line managers and other members of the company to listen to your new ideas and give them consideration. And you may have to negotiate for a lower price with suppliers. The most effective way to persuade and negotiate is to use down to earth language (no office jargon or sales jargon). Consider the situation from the point of view of the other person, and speak to what they feel about the situation more than what they think about it. The trick of negotiation and persuasion is to access the listener's emotions, which will positively influence their logical or intellectual view.

# EXAMPLE OF 'EMOTIONAL' PERSUASION OR NEGOTIATION.

A young Irishman who had what they call over there 'the gift of the gab' (able to chat and speak up for himself) attended an interview for a sales and marketing job. He chatted away through all of his questions, not being too casual but coming across as comfortable and relaxed at the same time.
The interviewers showed him two items and asked him which one he would market and sell.
1. A brand new teddy-bear or an old scrappy one, almost falling to pieces.
2. A large silver platter with beautiful engraving or a very plain silver platter with no carvings at all.

The interviewers watched him while Mark looked at all four objects, taking his time before answering. Eventually he was ready:
*"I would focus on selling the scrappy teddy-bear."*
*"Why not the brand new one?" the interviewers asked.*

*"Because when I look at the old teddy-bear it reminds me of the magical friendship with my teddy-bear that I had when I was a child. That flood of memories is likely to play on most parents' heartstrings before they consciously think about making a choice. I would find it much easier to sell a teddy-bear that has already had a long life as a child's comforter. And look at it… that toy needs to be homed once more before it falls apart completely. The new teddy bear hasn't been part of a child's growing-up yet, so it's a bit of a soul-less event waiting for something to happen to it."*

*"Fair enough", replied the interviewers. "Now, what about the silver platter?"*

*"That's an easy one", replied Mark. "The plain platter represents absolutely flawless craftsmanship. It is a symbol of quality and originality. The decorated platter looks more interesting, but if the craftsmanship in creating the platter has had flaws in it, the pattern/design serves a great purpose in concealing them.*

The interviewers told Mark that he had nearly reduced them to tears when he talked about how an old tattered teddy-bear has shared its life with a child as she grows up. So he had sold them on that one. His observations about the silver platter made them look at design and manufacture from an entirely new perspective, which they believed could progress their business. Mark was offered the job.

## You must be able to analyze situations appropriately

The interviewers will test your ability to do this by setting you hypothetical questions. To prepare for this, see the two examples below with some tips on how to think through a hypothetical dilemma.

Sample question: a demanding hypothetical situation:

So you've answered about your professional experience, your achievements and past work history. You are starting to feel more relaxed, when this curveball is thrown right into your lap:

> *You are driving in your two-seater sports car on a wild, stormy night. You pass a bus stop, and you see three people waiting for the bus:*
>
> *1. An old lady who looks as if she is might die.*

2. *An old friend who once saved your life.*
3. *The perfect man/woman you have been dreaming about meeting for years.*

Which one would you choose to offer a ride, knowing that there is only room for one passenger in your car? This is a moral dilemma question. Should you pick up the old lady? She is likely to die, you can't have that on your conscience knowing that you could have taken her somewhere safe, so should you save her first?

Or should you take your old friend? You are alive because of him – a huge gratitude to repay. This could go some way towards showing him how overwhelmed you still are by the generosity of his actions. But then, if you believe that the love-lightning strikes just once in a lifetime, you may never be able to find your perfect dream lover again if you pick up either of these.

A moral conundrum yes? Your chance to save a life, your chance to repay someone who saved your own life, or your chance to secure the partner of your dreams and enjoy a beautiful life together. Here's what the candidate chosen from 200 applicants: *"I would give my car keys to my old friend, and let him take the lady to the hospital. I would stay behind and wait for the bus with the woman of my dreams!"*

The real lesson of this answer is that if you are presented with a problem, of course you need to break it down to individual components to think it through, but your solution will often come by then bringing all those components back together. Maybe the order of a system needs to change. Maybe some staff roles need to change to find the perfect balance of skills that will solve the problem.

Here's another one:

*You are a shepherd bringing your flock to a warm, dry area away from the heavy rain. It is so heavy that a dam is on the verge of bursting. You come across the dam keeper with a broken leg, which happened while he was trying to reach the village below the dam to warn them of the danger. You have to get your flock of sheep in from the inclement weather. What would you do?"!*

**Don't panic!** Don't try to blurt out your answer. Take a few seconds to think - this shows confidence and assertiveness, and gives the interviewer a chance to see you in action thinking a problem through. Draw a quick diagram on your notebook if it helps you to see more clearly.

## You must have effective problem solving skills

This goes hand in hand with the guideline above, on analyzing situations properly. You analyze something either to understand it, explain it to someone else, or to solve a problem. Remember the three key stages:

- **Problem**
- **Action**
- **Outcome**

## You must be able to demonstrate drive and determination

If you have had a rough ride in life, you can bring up examples in the interview as to how you dealt with them because you have drive and determination. If you are going to use life experience examples, be sure to explain them from the perspective of a survivor who gained strength from sticking it out to the end. Don't tell the story from a 'victim' point of view.

## You must be able to work effectively in a team

Examples of school or university societies, group projects, or your professional experience of working with a team. Think of times when your team was so tight and supportive that every one of you enjoyed your job and worked really hard, often dealing with intense situations. Think of times when the sense of team was not good and explain the factors that you think caused this. The employer will not blame you for being part of a poor team spirit, they will value your analysis of what went wrong and how to address problems within a team.

## You must have a flexible attitude towards changing scenarios

Do you go with the flow or break in the wind? One of the most difficult things about being a professional is that usually, nothing goes exactly according to plan. So you need to have a good sense of lateral thinking and the ability to find detour routes if something changes dramatically in your situation. You then need to call on your negotiation and persuasion skills to bring your team on board with your suggested detour.

### You must have very good planning and organizing skills

Ok, so I've just said that most things don't go completely according to plan. But there has to be a plan to work from, a baseline upon which you can establish where every aspect of a task or project should be located in relation to each other. A good plan should be clear and easily explained, have a logical road-map of each stage, and a reasonable time schedule (with some leeway) for it to be completed with perfection.

### You must be able to see the bigger picture at all times

Again, look at the sample hypothetical questions below. My commentary about how to work out the best answer clearly demonstrates the need to be able to see the bigger picture. You can find many of these hypothetical questions online – they are good practice to get you thinking from a broader perspective.

### Don't try to form your whole answer immediately:

Just try to say one or two sensible things first. In the example above you might say that the moral dilemma is also an ethical one – do you place the welfare of animals on the same level as the welfare of another human being? For starters you could say that first you would examine the dam keeper's leg to see how bad the injury was. This gives you time to think further.

### There may be many possible solutions to the problem.

The interviewer won't be expecting a perfect answer. What you actually say in answer to a hypothetical question doesn't matter, so long as it sounds reasonable, confident and well thought out. It shows that you are bright, alert, and are aware of all of the issues involved.

### Creating the right impact with your overall impression

Just as there are several different ways an interviewer can ask you *"why do you think you are right for this job?"* We have several different ways in this book to revisit the fundamentals of giving what the interviewer is looking for. Interviewers are always searching for individuals who are self-motivated and enthusiastic, so get a good night's sleep the night before, and feel energized going into the interview. Most of the interviewers usually make up their mind on who to hire within ten to twenty minutes of the interview session. Because they judge you based on what you say and do within that time frame, it is therefore paramount that you put on an outstanding performance. Concentrate on making a great impression within the first few minutes and the interviewers may well warm up to you; this can make the rest of the interview much more enjoyable. But keep your guard up at all times – listen carefully to every question, and ensure to never interrupt an interviewer, and think before you speak!

## Speaking and listening – getting the balance right

Do look at the interviewer who is talking to you. Lean over slightly to show that you are paying attention. Probably about 80% of the time, this indicates that you are getting along with what they are saying. Anything short of this might make you come across as not really being interested in the interview. Nod your head at certain points while they speak, and repeat the occasional word or sentence to show that you are fully engaging with what they are saying to you.

## When to look away

Do look away at times while you are talking. If you aretrying to remember something you can look into the distance while you are thinking – give yourself a chance to get inside your head and into your memory store. It is actually a visual clue for the interviewer that you do retract into your own knowledge and understanding to try to come up with a solution to a problem.

## Special Focus D: Tell me about yourself

A lot of interviewers open the interview with this question, and it throws the floor open for you to say absolutely anything. This is exactly why it is a good idea to have a fairly fool-proof sense of what to say.

Don't take the question as a chance to pour out your entire life history. When you are asked this type of question interpret it as you are being asked to explain briefly a) your professional experience and b) why the qualities you possess are right for the role you applied for.

Summarize your work experience and the professional skills you have acquired. Concentrate on aspects of your experience that relate to the job. If marketing is a prerequisite for this job and you have marketing as part of your skills set, then make sure you focus on your experience in this field.

Don't ramble on, sharing some personal information about yourself with the interviewer like where you were born, how many of you are in your family, where you schooled, or what your parents do. It's not so much that this is the wrong answer, it just does little to sell yourself and your skills. If you've had some outstanding life experience that has given you determination of steel or links directly to the role you are applying for (such as nursing matched with caring for a seriously ill relative) these are examples of relevant skills that you can use.

You could also refer to your education and tell the interviewer where and what you studied – include notable snippets like your majors, significant awards or a distinction average, but only if the subjects you studied are relevant to the job. You may want to briefly describe why you chose your subject area and career path.

In all cases, stick to the point and make no more than four points in total. Don't waste time on irrelevant information – make sure that everything you say hits the mark for the job. Check with the job description and select four main aspects of the job that you could cover in the 'about yourself' answer.

## EXPLAINING YOUR STRENGTHS AND WEAKNESSES: MORE HELPFUL ACRONYMS

So we've had 'CCC' (well, not an acronym in the strictest sense), now let's take a look at CAR which stands for Challenge, Action and Result. This rule can apply to any question you are asked – if you can't put it across initially as a strength, use Challenge, Action and Result to explain:

> *"I was in a pickle (difficult situation), this is what I did to solve the pickle, this is how things turned out much for the better."*

More than meeting a candidate who can do everything, interviewers love a candidate who really can do everything. What this means is being able to turn a difficult situation into a challenge, take action, and show that the results have been positive. CAR will help you to construct great examples to back up your claims that you are as good as you say you are.

It will help if you try to explain the following points in your examples:

- **Challenge:** what was the problem that you turned into a challenge or an opportunity to solve? Set a very short scene for the story that you are about to tell and try to keep it as short as possible, ensuring that you point out the relevant skills they are looking for. Three or four sentences will be perfect.
- **Actions:** this part should be the bulk of your story, ensure that you use first person singular "I" rather than first person plural "We" to describe the action that you took i.e. the actions you took to resolve the problem. Again three or four sentences should be fine.
- **Result:** at this point, you need to explain the result of the actions you took. Generally, try to choose examples that describe successful outcomes.

Coming up with different examples for every skill that you may need to talk about in an interview can be really difficult, so you may end up using a handful of examples to demonstrate multiple skills. Write your challenges out beforehand and see which examples you can use that combine several of your most important skills. For instance, if you were involved in negotiating a deal with a difficult customer, you may have demonstrated skills which included researching the customer, writing a presentation and presenting it, putting together a business plan, and using outstanding customer service skills to keep them on board with you throughout. You can get away with referring back to the same example to illustrate different skills, but each time you do it, don't bore the interviewer by going through the entire CAR acronym. Just focus on the actions that you took to demonstrate that particular skill.

Finish off by briefly outlining how some of the most important challenges had a strong positive influence on your career plans, and how the job on offer fits calls on most of the skills you have outlined in your examples.

## So what are your strengths?

Doing the CAR preparation is likely to show you many strengths that you didn't realize you had. *"What are your strengths?"* is one of the next most popular questions that you will be asked at an interview, so take this opportunity to shine. This is yet another way of asking the question *"why do you think you are the right person for this job?"* You are being asked to explain why you are a great employee, how you can back up your brilliance with examples, and how your brilliance can be of immense benefit to the company. The best way to tackle this question is to return to the job description and note the key skills and characteristics the employer is looking for. Paraphrasing (repeating the context of these skills but in different terms) these back to the employer is a clever way to answer the question, because you are tapping into exactly what s/he wants to hear.

Examples of the skills that a recruiter most commonly seeks are:
- being able to thrive under pressure
- a great motivator
- a problem solver
- someone with extraordinary attention to detail
- A survivor against the toughest of odds
- Good at dealing with difficult people
- Strong communication skills

For instance, if project management is one of the requirements you can explain how you have managed projects or a team in the past, paying attention to your particular skills in this role. Explain the outcome of the project and what kind of experience it was for the team (emphasizing on what you did to make it a positive experience). Illustrate how your team were appreciative of having such a strong plan to work with on the project, and how well they felt supported by you. Do also refer to time management, explaining that the project was delivered within the predicted time frame and indicate what % of money you saved for the company.

Organize your answers around some of the following strengths:

*"My time management skills are excellent. In fact, in my last job I boosted productivity in my team by 30%, and cut absenteeism down by 40%. This was just by reorganizing and re-distributing the workload, and giving my staff-team realistic goals and deadlines."*

*"I'm organized and take pride in excelling at my work."*

*"I'm very good with customers and I am efficient at resolving any problems they may have. My communication skills help me both to get along with my team-members and to deliver excellent customer service."*

*"I respond well to pressure and am able to prioritize my work well."*

Don't forget to ensure that your body language demonstrates each point you make. Look enthusiastic and positive while you describe your strengths – this is your chance to shine, and an interviewer will become suspicious if you don't seem animated when you have the chance to talk about your strengths, which make any job enjoyable.

### And what are your weaknesses?

So here's the other side of the coin! If you are asked about your strengths, they will most certainly ask about your weaknesses too. The key to answering this question is not to respond literally. Your future employer most likely won't care if your weak spot is that you can't cook, nor do they want to hear the generic responses, like you're "too detail oriented" or "work too hard." We all have more weaknesses than we can count, which is not to say that we are rubbish at doing things, but simply that out of everything we do in life, there are aspects that we are not so good at. Discuss only what is relevant to the job you are applying for.

Respond to this query by identifying areas in your work that you can improve, and figure out how turning these weaknesses into strengths can be assets to a future employer. One word of importance though – if your weaknesses make you unsuitable for the job, don't try to push yourself into the wrong position. Our weaknesses include many of the things that are not our strengths. In other words, you can't be good at everything, you'll be 'so-so' at other things, and some of your weaknesses will always remain weaknesses. It's a good idea to check yourself against the requirements of the job and if they match with too many of your weaknesses and not enough of your strengths, save yourself the injury of trying to squeeze into it. Something that you are much more suited to will soon come along.

If you didn't have the opportunity to develop certain skills at your previous job, explain how eager you are to gain that skill in a new position. This is not really stating a weakness; you are simply explaining an area that has not yet become a strength. As long as you don't need extensive training to gain this skill and feel sure that you can develop it quickly through on-the-job experience, it's fine to bring it up at the interview.

If you say that you don't have any weaknesses the interviewer will immediately see you as being guarded – so guarded that you are willing to lie about having any weaknesses. Anyone who is human and not a robot has weaknesses! No-one is perfect at everything. Just keep your CAR formula in mind. For example, if the job requires face to face contact with customers and colleagues, then you can say that you get bored easily when you have to spend a lot of time on your own. So you respond with a weakness that will transform into a strength within the new job role. Another example might be: *"In my previous job, being able to develop my public-speaking skills was challenging. I'd really like to be able to work in a place that will give me the opportunity to give presentations and talk in front of others."*

When discussing your weaknesses, always explain how you compensate for them. Describe the actions or steps that you will take to ensure that your weaknesses don't affect your performance at work.

Here's another example:

*"I've been told I occasionally focus on details and miss the bigger picture, so I've been spending time laying out the complete project every day to see my overall progress."*

## How do you work under pressure?

Neither work nor life come free of pressures. For most employers, the perfect candidate is someone who is able to work under pressure, who neither explodes at other people when pressurized, or who visible shakes when stressed. Does this describe a superhuman? Well yes and no. Some people are entirely calm during pressure because this is how they thrive at work. Others lose all their focus when the pressure heats up. Most people fall somewhere between the two. Employers don't want to work with someone who loses their cool or is at risk of 'going over the edge' under pressure.

'Calm' is the key word – regardless of what you feel inside, what you need to communicate to the employer is that although you feel the stress of being under pressure, your strategy to get through it is to assess the situation, reorganize yourself, stay focused and get the work done to a high standard. Delivering less than satisfactory work just to get through the pressured situation is worse than not delivering it at all, because it's very hard to rectify a project once it has been completed shoddily. You can say that everyone has their weaknesses, and they are certainly tested under pressure. For that reason you will always involve other people in trying to find a solution rather than try and fail to deliver to your usual high standard, all by yourself.

Describe a situation when you were under pressure and detail how you approached the situation and managed to organize, mobilize and deliver a good result. If you're someone who actually performs better when under pressure, then good for you. If the reverse is the case don't worry, all hope is not lost. You can also say that you try as much as possible to avoid creating pressure-filled situations by being super-organized and giving yourself lots of lead time. This enables you to be as well-prepared as possible and gives you excellent prioritization insight. Also, if a crisis does happen, you are good at pulling your team-members together to deal with it methodically, so that the pressure is shared and halved across everyone's shoulders.

You can also describe a situation from your personal life where you exhibited grace under pressure. Highlight the positive qualities you demonstrated in the situation, which could have been the ability to calm and motivate others, or communicate clearly. Some jobs are inherently pressure filled by nature, so make sure you're going for a job you can handle. If dealing with pressure isn't your thing, you might want to reconsider your move into a career that is very deadline-driven or where you're under constant pressure to produce and deliver. Remember, finding the right job is all about finding the right fit between your strengths and personality; the worst injustice you could do to yourself is to go for a job you don't enjoy. Life is too short to have to cope through a job instead of enjoying through.

### The "Silent Treatment"

**TRAPS:** Beware – if you are unprepared for this question, you will probably not handle it right and possibly blow the interview. Thank goodness most interviewers don't employ it. It's normally used by those determined to see how you respond under stress.

Here's how it works: You answer an interviewer's question and then, instead of asking another, he just stares at you in a deafening silence. You wait, growing a bit uneasy, and there he sits, silent as Mt. Rushmore, as if he doesn't believe what you've just said, or perhaps making you feel that you've unwittingly violated some cardinal rule of interview etiquette.

When you get this silent treatment after answering a particularly difficult question, such as "tell me about your weaknesses", its intimidating effect can be most disquieting, even to polished job hunters. Most unprepared candidates rush in to fill the void of silence, viewing prolonged, uncomfortable silences as an invitation to clear up the previous answer which has obviously caused some problem. And that's what they do – ramble on, sputtering more and more information, sometimes irrelevant and often damaging, because they are suddenly playing the role of someone who's goofed and is now trying to recoup. But since the candidate doesn't know where or how he goofed, he just keeps talking, showing how flustered and confused he is by the interviewer's unmovable silence.

BEST ANSWER: Like a primitive tribal mask, the Silent Treatment loses all its power to frighten you once you refuse to be intimidated. If your interviewer pulls it, keep quiet yourself for a while and then ask, with sincere politeness and not a trace of sarcasm, "Is there anything else I can fill in on that point?" That's all there is to it. Whatever you do, don't let the Silent Treatment intimidate you into talking a blue streak, because you could easily talk yourself out of the position.

## MORE TYPICAL INTERVIEW QUESTIONS

### What motivates you?

This question is more than just an interview question – it's something every job seeker should ask themselves before embarking on their job quest. The clearer you are about this, the better you will be able to articulate it to a prospective employer – and the closer you will get to land your dream job. Don't just memorize one of these answers by heart. Take a moment to figure out what really motivates you – you'll sound much more genuine.

Most employers are looking for people who are eager to make a difference to their organisation. So if perhaps the only thing that keeps you going is the thought of leaving work at the end of the day, honestly, keep that to yourself – it will kill what might have been an otherwise brilliant interview for you. It may be wise to say something along the lines of:

- you are motivated by the opportunities that you can pursue in life
- you want to be recognized for a job well done
- you don't feel fulfilled when a customer leaves unsatisfied
- you enjoy pushing others as well as yourself

### Other good answers include:

**Recognition:** while employers consider it awkward to hear that you are motivated by money, you can rephrase it in a different way such as: you like to have your good work recognized by your boss, peers or clients.

**A good work/life balance:** some candidates worry that this is the worst thing they could possibly say in an interview. It's not. All you are doing is telling them that you work to the absolute best of your ability, but in order to stay fresh and full of good ideas, that 'life' time outside of work to do things is also of great importance. The firm will respect you for setting this boundary, unless you are applying to work in investment banking, where you have to be ready to sign your time away to 100 hour weeks. This is the exception however; most companies want their staff to have regular 'switch-off' time. If you don't get it outside of work, how on earth are you to be energized and alert at work. Good companies want their staff to be fresh and happy.

Making a difference: Especially in the charity or non-profit sector, saying that you are motivated by the pursuit of the organization's goals is a good point. Make sure to have read their mission statement and know what their goals are.

**Challenge:** Another good answer is to say that you enjoy getting fully involved in solving problems and getting to the bottom of difficult situations.

Self-development: Employers like candidates who want to further their own learning and development. Do bear in mind the nature of the role that you are applying for, though. A management training scheme is likely to provide you with much more by way of development opportunities than, say, an office data entry job.

**Money:** Only when going for a sales job should you talk about the fact that you are motivated by financial reward.

In fact, many sales people are suspicious of candidates who say that they are not motivated by money and the luxuries that money can allow you to buy. It's vital to give the interviewer an idea of who you are and what makes you tick – but to present yourself in the most positive light possible.

**Tell me how you can effectively manage your time**

A lot of employers, especially those who seek to fill high profile roles are looking for impeccable time management skills. They want to know how efficient you can be with the responsibilities you will be entrusted with, and whether you can differentiate between what needs to be done immediately and what can wait for another few hours. A good way to answer this sort of question is to say that you make sure that first things come first, i.e. you prioritize the most and urgent tasks to the top of the pile, and then prioritize in order your list of 'important but not urgent' tasks. You always try to get all the work done and not allow a backlog to form, even if it means that you have to stay late sometimes. Citing an example of how and when you demonstrated this skill, will be a plus.

Try and illustrate your organizational skills by talking about some of the methods or systems that you use to organize your work, such as:

- Making lists of tasks
- Keeping files and records on different projects
- Developing a routine or process
- Using tables, spreadsheets, computer programs
- Using Gantt charts (but only talk about these last two points if you genuinely have used them) to track progress on different pieces of work

**How would you describe your people skills?**

If employers had to pick the most important category of skills in choosing between candidates, they'd probably pick interpersonal skills. Unless you are working in a sealed room without even a telephone in it (which is a highly unlikely situation) you'll need good inter-personal skills to deal with colleagues, clients, customers, suppliers, and anyone else that you liaise with in your role. In particular roles, such as sales, you may need highly developed pitching and negotiation skills. But the questions in this section are relevant to just about everyone.

- **Do you prefer to work on your own or in a team?**
  Team working skills are highly prized in most organizations. At the same time though, don't imply that you are completely hopeless and unable to concentrate when a task requires you to work independently of others. This question has no single right answer. Your approach to the question depends on the nature of the job. Take a few seconds to think about how much time the job would require you to spend working in a team versus working on your own.

- **How would you describe your current boss?**

  This is the king of interpersonal skills questions – the recruiter wants to know what your relationship is like with your current boss. If they are difficult, how do you manage to communicate effectively with them? If they are very approachable, do you still maintain professional boundaries and not become too familiar with them?

Depending on the interviewer, you might get away with pointing out some not very good aspects of your previous boss but you will be treading on dangerous ground if you disparage your boss. Never, ever talk badly about your past bosses; just explain some of the challenges of working with them if you have had to overcome them in order to perform at your best in your job. A potential boss will anticipate that you'll talk about him or her in the same manner somewhere down the line, so be as sensible and transparent as possible. Don't leave the interviewer wondering if any of the fault is on your part.

To balance the scales on this one, always be positive about your current manager's abilities. Have much more positive to say about them than negative. At the same time, don't make your boss sound too fantastic –especially if the interviewers are your prospective employer – you might make them feel insecure or inadequate (Yes, really!).

With this question, the interviewer is also looking for a cultural fit. If your potential boss is your interviewer, he/she will be looking for answers that show you are easy to work with and that you are a strong contributor to your team. Emphasize ways in which you interact with your current boss in your working environment to achieve the goals of the business. Show how this will help you in the new role you are applying for.

**Suggested Answers:**

*"My boss gives me a lot of latitude in how I work; we try to tackle problems together. He trusts me completely, so it's refreshing not to be micro-managed at all. All in all, he's a good manager to work for."*

*"I have a very good boss; he takes time out to understand what I want out of my career and has given me tasks that help me to achieve my goal of moving into a customer-facing role. He is also very understanding."*

*"My boss would tell you that I am good at coming up with solutions that are a little out of the box, which often give us the edge over our competitors. I'm also a good implementer so when she has decided on a way forward, she can trust me to implement it well."*

*"While none of my past bosses were awful, there are some who taught me more than others did. I've definitely learned what types of management styles I work with the best."*

## Describe a time when you were faced with a difficult situation and how you handled it

This is a very tricky question; you need to pause and think before answering this question. You need to think of a time you faced a significant challenge and how you successfully resolved it or overcame it. If you have a significant life experience that proved you to have more resilience than you ever thought yourself capable, this is a good life example that shows that whatever skills you possess in a professional sense, you bear them out in your personal life too. It shows that you are consistent, and it tells the employer that s/he can believe in your professional strengths, because they are true of your personal integrity too.

The interviewer is also trying to determine what you define as 'difficult', so try to choose an example that was challenging but not impossible to resolve. And you can choose an example that has some considerable weight to it rather than using something trivial. Here are some examples:

- Being made unemployed because of redundancy when your company downsized, and how you sought out temporal jobs that kept you financially afloat while you applied for a job that meets your qualifications.
- A contract falling through at the last minute, and having to do the work yourself

- An unexpected major event that threw your life plans into disarray, and how you got things back on track
- how you dealt with client requests to meet tight (or impossible!) deadlines

The interviewer wants to see that you have resilience, problem-solving skills, initiative and the ability to work around less-than desirable situations. Clearly explain (again, be brief but accurate with how you tell the story) how you faced up to the challenge by adopting a strong, positive attitude and what the final positive outcome was. Keep in mind they are interested in determining how your actions and decisions will affect the business, so even if you are describing a challenging life situation, always describe a conclusion that shows you acting with skills that can be transferred to your professional role with their company.

### Aren't you overqualified for this position?

The employer may be concerned that you'll grow dissatisfied and leave.

BEST ANSWER: As with any objection, don't view this as a sign of imminent defeat. It's an invitation to teach the interviewer a new way to think about this situation, seeing advantages instead of drawbacks. Example: "I recognize the job market for what it is – a marketplace. Like any marketplace, it's subject to the laws of supply and demand. So 'overqualified' can be a relative term, depending on how tight the job market is. And right now, it's very tight. I understand and accept that. ""I also believe that there could be very positive benefits for both of us in this match. ""Because of my unusually strong experience in _____, I could start to contribute right away, perhaps much faster than someone who'd have to be brought along more slowly." "There's also the value of all the training and years of experience that other companies have invested tens of thousands of dollars to give me. You'd be getting all the value of that without having to pay an extra dime for it. With someone who has yet to acquire that experience, he'd have to gain it on your nickel." "I could also help you in many things they don't teach at the Harvard Business School. For example (how to hire, train, motivate, etc.) When it comes to knowing how to work well with people and getting the most out of them, there's just no substitute for what you learn over many years of front-line experience. Your company would gain all this, too. ""From my side, there are strong benefits, as well. Right now, I am unemployed.

I want to work, very much, and the position you have here is exactly what I love to do and I'm best at. I'll be happy doing this work and that's what matters most to me, a lot more than money or title. ""Most importantly, I'm looking to make a long term commitment in my career now. I've had enough of job-hunting and want a permanent spot at this point in my career. I also know that if I perform this job with excellence, other opportunities cannot help but open up for me right here. In time, I'll find many other ways to help this company and in so doing, help myself. I really am looking to make a long-term commitment.

"NOTE: The main concern behind the "overqualified" question is that you will leave your new employer as soon as something better comes your way. Anything you can say to demonstrate the sincerity of your commitment to the employer and reassure them that you're looking to stay for the long-term will help you overcome this objection

## What did you most enjoy about your last or current job?

If you are going for a job in sales, it would be a good idea to emphasize your love of client interaction and negotiating and closing a deal. If the position you apply for requires you to meet important deadlines, you could highlight that you thrive when working in a high-pressure environment.

And just to reiterate that all-important word of warning – it's better to talk about liking challenges and achievements. If your team and manager were a joy to work with, mention this and say that you really value having supportive, stimulating team-members and management around you. If you are a 'peoples' person describe how you found client contact to be one of the most enjoyable parts of your job.

Only the sales industry will be impressed with you talking about clinching a profitable sale, and don't mention liking the long corporate lunches! (If they're your idea of hell, don't mention that either.)

# CHAPTER 5:

# TAILORING THE INTERVIEW

Now that you've done your lifetime's worth of general interview preparation it's time to tailor your interview towards the very company that you are applying to. This chapter looks at how to research the company in detail and base your answers on what you find out about it. Just as there's nothing to be gained by submitting a generic CV/Resume, there's equally nothing to be gained by preparing generic answers to apply to any interview.

## ABOUT THE COMPANY

Ensure you've done all your homework well before the day. Whatever position you are applying for, be it the VP of marketing, a hospital ward manager, or a sales assistant, you should know about the company or organisation that you want to work for. Their particular position within the industry will have characteristics that make its unique from other similar positions. Knowing what these shows that you are serious and keen to be part of their team. It will come across clearly to them that you are not applying for *a* job … you are applying for *this* job.

Use internet search engines to find reviews, news features or other websites that come up when you search for the company name as this is more reliable information generated by others, and not the company singing its own praises. At the interview, you can discuss a number of aspects such as services, goals, position in the market and other points that you have gleaned from your research. Make sure you show knowledge without coming across as a 'know-all'. Here's an example of not going overboard: *"I was impressed with your growth figures over the past twelve months and it's great that you have a policy to support the local community"*. This answer shows you have done your homework and gives the company a pat on the back for their social policies.

## WHY DO YOU WANT TO WORK FOR OUR COMPANY?

This should be directly related to the last question. Any research you've done on the company should have led you to the conclusion that you'd want to work there. After all, you're at the interview, right? Put some thought into this answer before you have your interview, mention your career goals and highlight forward-thinking goals and career plans.

## WHY ARE YOU APPLYING FOR THIS JOB?

This is another tricky question but it's easier to answer correctly if you bear in mind that the employer wants to know one thing: are you applying for this job because of the money or because you really are serious about the company? When you answer this question, use your answer to build on your knowledge of the company and re-emphasize why you are the best candidate for the position you are applying for. Ensure you give examples of what attracted you to the company so that the interviewer can see that you really do match their advertised role and will thrive in their culture.

> *While this looks like a question about you, the interviewer wants to know what you can do for the company and that you are a good fit for the job.*

In your answer, you might want to elaborate on your strengths and achievements and how they match the position description. You could also talk about your career goals and the objectives of the company (information from your research). In both of these instances, you are explaining how and why you would be an asset to the company.

**What relevant experience do you have?**

My guess is that since you have made it to the interview, you already have bags of experience in relation to the role you are applying for. This question can pull the rug from under your feet because it so directly requires you to repeat what is in your CV/Resume. Don't be fooled into abbreviating your answer, thinking that you've already given this information more extensively in your application. Mention all of your most significant experience – the more you can link to the job, the better your chances of being offered it.

If for instance you are switching careers or trying something different from what you used to do, much of your experience might not match up so you need to be very aware of linking everything that has given you transferable skills. Take your time and figure out how you can match up your existing experience with what the current job required. There are many skills common to most jobs.

**For example:**
- communication skills
- being a good team-member
- being a fair and popular senior manager
- having good time management and organizational skills
- excellent crisis manager

# HOW DO YOU DEAL WITH PROBLEMS?

Problems are sure to arise on a day to day basis not just at work but guaranteed in general life too. Interviewers want employees who know how to tackle life challenges and deal with problems calmly and effectively. For the best employees, every problem has a solution and no obstacle is insurmountable.

To show your prospective employer your can-do attitude, you want to demonstrate that your approach to problem-solving is calm, rational and objective. Be ready to explain that your approach is to break down a problem into its component parts so you can see the main issues and what exactly needs to be done. Also be able to identify the cause of the problem, which will help to figure out where to start solving it. Then do whatever research is required and brainstorm possible solutions, both alone and with others. If appropriate, you assemble the necessary team. Organize yourself, reset your current priorities if you need to, and set yourself a strategy and schedule. Tackle the problem straight away instead of procrastinating, as procrastination is guaranteed to elaborate the problem. Be resourceful and resilient, and not afraid to be creative and innovative in your approach. For you, there are only challenges, not problems.

Most importantly, you need to demonstrate all these claims with a concrete example from your past, professional or personal life. Outline the nature of the problem, how you approached and assessed it, what actions you took, and the result of your actions – in other words, how you overcame the problem. If you really want to impress your interviewer, cite an example of how, through your foresight and initiative, you were able to anticipate and prevent a potential problem before it arose. In other words, you are proactive rather than merely reactive, and you always look ahead and do your best to cover all the bases. With this approach you can't go wrong. Your interviewer is sure to be convinced that you've got the right stuff to be an indispensable member of their team.

### Describe a time when you have worked as part of a successful team. What do you think contributed to your team's overall success?

Now that all onsite jobs require you to work in teams, this is a commonly asked question. Working in a team is a critical factor that ensures the smooth running of any business. Employers will always want to know that you have experience of working in cohesive and successful team environments, outside of work as well as at work.

Even if you haven't worked before, I'm sure you would have done some kind of collaborative work with others, whether it be projects at school or university with friends, or working on some kind of project with your local community. Ensure that you give an example of a time or times that you have worked in a team and discuss the outcome of the experience. You can choose to discuss a work assignment or an extracurricular activity, so long as you have had extensive contact with your fellow team-members. Paint the interviewer a picture by describing the scenario and the details of the personalities and roles in your team.

When answering this question, ensure that you talk about the role you played and what contributions you made to the team that made it successful. You will need to find the balance between portraying yourself as doing too much and doing too little, in order to avoid the unwanted labels of slacker or control freak. Be sure to mention the qualities and strengths that you drew on to accomplish the task. Don't be afraid to mention any weaknesses you faced and how you worked through them.

It is important for you to discuss the strategy your team put in place to ensure that everyone worked together effectively and the success achieved. How was the leader appointed? Who appointed the leader or were each of you given charge of different tasks? Discuss whatever you think will be useful to project you in a good light, no matter how trivial it might seem. Also feel free to mention any challenges or obstacles that you had along the way and how you worked together to overcome them.

Sum up your answer by saying what you learnt from the experience. This is more important than the quantifiable success of your team. Showing the interviewer that you have reflected and learnt from this experience shows that you are a mature and adaptable worker, and hopefully just the applicant they are looking for.

## DESCRIBE A SITUATION WHERE YOU HAD TO DEAL WITH A DIFFICULT PERSON.

Ah, here's a tricky question to navigate. All of us have had to deal with difficult people at some point in our lives; we have all had different upbringings, so we tend to act differently in different interpersonal situations. Our history of encountering difficult people may have been at work, at school, or even in our own families. How you deal with such people says a lot about you to potential employers, and may be the deciding factor about whether or not you will fit into a particular organization's culture, which is made up of a whole complex of different personalities.

Conflict is never desirable in the workplace but is bound to occur occasionally, so employers are looking for someone who generally gets along with others. If you have something in particular to say about yourself (that is positive) about how you deal with conflict, do bring it up at the interview when you are answering this question. Employers look for someone who can demonstrate diplomacy and calmness when dealing with difficult people. The ideal personality they have in mind is someone who is not argumentative or overly sensitive, who is good at defusing tense situations and knows when to compromise at the same time remaining professional.

People who are natural diplomats and mediators are valuable assets to any company, so if you can think of a situation where you were faced with a difficult or angry person and were able to calm them down, talk them through the situation and turn them around with your delicate powers of persuasion, then that will surely impress your interviewer. It's not necessary to be a doormat and there are times when it's important to assert yourself and stand up for what you believe in. However, it's always important to remain calm, rational and reasonable, and to respect other people's views. An employee who displays such quality is worth their weight in gold and will be much sought after.

## WHY DID YOU LEAVE YOUR LAST JOB?

The key to answering this particular question is to maintain a positive attitude, no matter what the reason is. You may have left as a result of an argument with your boss but it's important that you maintain a positive outlook towards the situation. A sure-fire way to teleport your application to the bottom of the pile is to badmouth your ex-boss and grumble about your old job. Save that for when you've got time to have a long, uninterrupted rant with your partner or your friends.

Be clear, confident and calm about why you left, or are leaving, your previous job, and back this up by redirecting your response to exactly why you are so keen to work in the position on offer. Below are some reasons for leaving a job. Be as honest as possible, there is no point cooking up some lies because this can almost certainly backfire later in the future.

**Reasons for leaving**

You got sacked: This is a very difficult honest answer to give because so many questions arise out of it, but it's important to hold your cool and don't panic. Stay as honest as possible, take responsibility for the situation, explain what you have learned from the experience and how the problem won't apply to the new position. If you are caught lying, your chances will go up in smoke.

Possible response: *"It was decided that my skills and qualifications weren't suited to the position. I am excited by this role because it matches my experience and I know I will be able to thrive and make a valuable contribution to the company."*

**You were made redundant:** This question will become more common as the economy continues to slow down. It's a tough question, however, especially because many workers aren't told exactly why they were laid off. The best way to tackle this question is to answer as honestly as possible. Being made redundant is a world away from getting sacked. Make sure you explain the circumstances behind the redundancy – the company was downsizing, moving in a different direction or relocating to another state. This will reassure your interviewers that the decision was in no way based on your ability or attitude. However, don't dwell on it – nothing screams 'don't hire me' like a bitter or insecure mind-set. Don't feel that you need to explain yourself over and over. Show that you are enthusiastic about the career opportunities you are now presented with and are ready for new challenges. Possible response 1: *"As I'm sure you're aware, the economy is tough right now and my company* *felt the effects of it. I was part of a large staff reduction and that's really all I know. I am confident, however, that it had nothing to do with my job performance, as exemplified by my accomplishments. For example..."*

Possible response 2: *"The Company was relocating to Abuja and closing my branch. I had been with the company for seven years and I see this as a fantastic opportunity to use the skills I gained in that time in a new role."*

**You hated your boss/colleagues/job/all of the above:** Despising the ground your boss walks on, wanting to strangle your colleagues or an inexplicably tedious job are very valid reasons for quitting. But offload your career angst on your family members or friends and make sure the angry vibes get nowhere near the interview hot seat. Focus on other reasons, any other reasons, about why you are considering a change of job and psych yourself into a positive frame of mind.

Possible response: *"After graduating, I spent five years with one company gaining exceptional knowledge of the industry. I am now enthusiastic to apply my skills in a different organisation with new opportunities and challenges."*

**You weren't getting paid enough:** This is a very honest answer to give but the bottom line is that it's not an impressive reason for you to leave your job, especially when a particular pay had been agreed on. It also won't go down well if it becomes evident that you have an over-inflated sense of your own monetary value – and that they will be funding your next round-the-world trip! You can mention that your previous employer wasn't doing well enough to pay competitive rates, but make sure you balance up your answer with a more optimistic reason for pursuing a new path.

Possible response: *"The company was going through a difficult financial patch and were unable to pay competitive rates and keep up with evolving technology. With 10 years of accounting experience, an MBA and a young family, I would like to work for a dynamic organisation that has a solid future."*

**The job wasn't stimulating enough:**

Once you feel trapped or frustrated in a job, perhaps it's time for you to move on/up in your career. It is a smart career move to see what else is out there for you and what opportunities can open up for you.

However, you have to be very careful while phrasing your answer or the interviewer might be left with the impression that you are easily bored and unmotivated. Instead, focus on your excitement and enthusiasm for the job they are offering, referring to specifics, and illustrating your qualifications.

Possible response: *"I had a rewarding seven years at my former company and was involved with projects I am immensely proud of, but when I saw the advertisement for this position I knew it was a perfect match for my skills and couldn't resist applying."*

## Change of life circumstances

One of the major reasons people leave their old job is due to personal issues or circumstances. Marriage, for example, might necessitate a move to a different part of the country, or a need for a higher income job. Telling the interviewer that you left your old job because the new one is streets away doesn't paint you in a reliable picture of drive and motivation!

Possible response: *"I took five years off from my last position because I had two daughters. They are now in primary school and I am excited to move back into full-time work, especially into a position like this where I will be able to make a valuable contribution to a company I have always admired."*

## What characteristics do you think make a successful manager?

This question always comes when you are applying for a senior or managerial role; your prospective employer will want to know your view on how to manage people or oversee a task. When you move into a management position your 'hands-on' knowledge of the industry takes a back seat to how well you can lead people and make them feel a valued part of the team.

Managing people often depends on your personality, the culture of the company, (because companies have different ways of running a business and managing their staff). Some roles require strong decisive leadership, while others benefit from a more collaborative, consultative style. So there is no particular strict way of managing people. Be on the lookout for the type of job that is advertised as managerial, but in actuality you yourself are being micro-managed and pushed into leading your team according the an aggressive set of values. If you can't use your own initiative and lead people with your values and qualities, the job is managerial only by name. You should be supported in a management role, not dictated to.

The best managers are known to be flexible and are able to modify their approach depending on the circumstance and the people or company they are dealing with. This is as much about your own line managers as it is about how you manage your team of staff. Below are some characteristics which most successful managers possess:

- Trustworthy and open
- Clear communicator – you are approachable in giving feedback and instructions to your staff, and listening to them and their concerns.
- Positive and encouraging
- Calm and reasonable
- You provide clear direction and have reasonable expectations
- Flexible and reasonable
- Hard-working but know when your staff need to pace themselves
- Strategic in vision with logical problem-solving skills
- Decisive
- Well-informed and knowledgeable about the business

**Exercise**

Take a pencil now and write down four of the characteristics from this list that you feel most apply to you. Think of situations when you have successfully demonstrated these qualities, and if you have been promoted to a more senior role in previous jobs because you demonstrated your leadership skills so effectively. Expand on why you think they're important, how they will be relevant to the role you are applying for, and how you have demonstrated these qualities in the past. You could also describe how a previous manager of yours displayed these qualities to good effect, and how you learned from that example. This is a particularly good way to round off this question – it shows that you have the ability to recognize best practice in leaders and managers throughout your work history, and to adopt their style into your own. Can you describe a time when you have taken initiative?

## What was the result?

With this question the interviewer wants to test if you can think on your feet; it's one of the more tricky aspects of being in any employment, that you will be faced with situations that require you to think on your feet, so having the ability to remain calm, see clearly and take the initiative is very essential. When you answer this question be sure to give examples of a time or times when you have come up with an idea and how you went about seeing it through to completion. Talk about the challenges you faced throughout the whole process and how you overcame these to succeed. Maybe you came up with an idea for a new project which would cost the company minimal overheads but create maximum profits. If you have experience of presenting business proposals to put forth new ideas, this shows that you have the skills to present an idea successfully in writing, which you then follow up verbally by presenting it to the board. If the idea is taken up and then successfully carried out, this shows that you can bring valuable skills to the job such as leadership, motivation and problem solving, and negotiation with possible new business prospects.

Also, try to emphasize the importance of teamwork. For example, you could emphasize that *"While I have the ability to take direction and work on my own, I am also an excellent team player and I firmly believe in working together to obtain the best possible results as a group."*

## Why did you choose this career path?

As broad as this question is, you should have a well-tailored answer for it. Your motive while discussing this should be to demonstrate to your prospective employer that you are focused, know what you want, and have a genuine passion for your chosen industry.

You must have specific reason for choosing your particular career path; this shows that you are dedicated and keen about the job you are applying for. Ensure to point out aspects of your personality, interests or significant experiences from your personal or professional past that has helped to steer you in your present direction. This has to be about you and your choices and aspirations; citing reasons of money, status or that your parents made you do it won't do much to advance your cause – demonstrating genuine passion for the career path you are pursuing will.

Show the interviewer that you and the position you are applying for are a perfect fit. If you are applying for a job in public relations you could say:

*"I've always been a strong communicator and people person. I also like a fast-paced, high-energy environment so a career in PR is a natural path for me."*

With such an open-ended question, there is always the danger of trying to pack your whole life's history into it. Be specific, and elaborate. You don't have to answer in monosyllables but refrain from rambling on too much too. Don't give long and boring answers – be direct and to-the point. Pick one main reason why you chose the career path and elaborate with a few specific points that link your experience and pursuit of this path with the job requirements). Show the interviewer that your skills and personality are exactly what the company needs.

### How do you handle criticism?

This question needs to be handled cleverly. You need to put across that you can deal with criticism, accept it when it is due but are also assertive enough to challenge if it is inappropriate. If you navigate it with a lot of personal awareness and tact it *is* possible to answer without perjuring yourself. Every employee has to accept criticism at some point or another, so as long as you are open and honest without giving anything away that might raise alarm bells for the employer. Here are some suggestions as to how you can answer this question:

### "I see criticism as an opportunity to improve my work"

Try to show the interviewer that you are more than happy to put your ego aside and take corrections. You need to realize that constructive criticism is an important part of professional growth. This is also an opportunity to show your employer that you are striving to be the best and are ready to improve yourself. Criticism can cause pangs for us all, until the intellect kicks in and makes sense of it as professional direction and guidance. In your job, as long as criticism is not personal and is directed to something that you could have done better, just take it as feedback and advice. It should never make you feel bad about yourself – take professional criticism instead as an agent for change when it happens.

### "I decide whether the criticism is valid or not"

Now not all criticisms are as important as people perceive them to be; some people dole out criticism because it is their way to criticize unnecessarily. You need to judge this for yourself on its own merits. Weigh up what has been said to you with how you normally respond to instruction and your shrewd judgement to decide whether it is just or not. After weighing up the evidence, you may decide that you are actually making the correct decision. If criticism springs from a person's doubt about your abilities, jealousy of your success or pure nastiness, it will have a different tone to it and certainly won't come across as being helpful instruction or feedback. Be strong and confident in your abilities – most successful people in life are those who go against the grain to achieve what they are truly passionate about.

### "It depends on whether the criticism is from a colleague or a client"

While customer satisfaction is of utmost importance to every business, there are times when you need to differentiate between whether to take it seriously or not. How you react depends on how sensibly you interpret what has been said to you, and whether it's something that you need to take on board. In life, more's the pity, there are always people who complain and find fault. Whether they be customers, colleagues or employers we can all fall foul of them at some point or another.

If you are going for a job as a waiter or restaurant manager, the interviewer will want to know how you would handle a cranky customer. If you are an airline check-in steward, how you would diffuse the situation if flights were delayed and passengers are in a panic to get home? Criticism from a client differs greatly from that of your colleague, so both shouldn't carry the same weight. A colleague knows your work and personality and works alongside you every day, so their criticism is likely to be constructive and intended to be helpful. In other words, it is more than definitely likely to be professional rather than personal.

At the same time, how you deal with difficult or critical customers all falls back to your communication skills. You have to assess whether they have a valid point or not, and you need to have a way of placating them tactfully even if they *are* just blowing hot air. Your potential employer won't be impressed at the thought of you publicly arching your back at the gall of a customer lodging a legitimate complaint. On the other hand, they will also expect you to diplomatically defend their business if the customer is not being reasonable.

What you need to stress overall is that you are always open to criticism from your manager if it is intended to help you develop your role and broaden your range of skills. The best of us consciously learn from making mistakes and going back over the same task at the next opportunity putting good advice and guidance into practice.

**Give an example**

So here's where you have to put your money where your mouth is, and prove that you have examples to back up what you have just said about how you receive criticism. It is always good to give real-life examples especially because they prove to your prospective employer that your answer is based on who you actually are, rather than a character you have created for them because you naturally want to storm the interview. Be sure to give as many examples as possible, with a mix of criticism from your boss, your colleagues, and some clients. If you need to choose some examples from an environment that is not work-related, do so. Describe how you viewed the criticism objectively, how you took ownership of the problem and how that improved your work. If you are in a leadership position, you will need to show that you are responsive to criticism by calling a meeting to discuss feedback and work towards new solutions.

The dos and don'ts of hearing what you don't want to hear:

- Do listen objectively
- Do ask for specifics

- Do get a second opinion and do your own research
- Do take ownership and responsibility
- Do take feedback into consideration
- Do learn from it
- Don't ignore the criticism
- Don't get defensive, angry or rude
- Don't make excuses
- Don't dwell on the error

# WHERE DO YOU SEE YOURSELF IN LIFE IN FIVE YEARS?

This is when you have to use this opportunity to highlight your ambitions and your dedication to the industry, so that your prospective employers don't think you will run away after few months of working with them. Answer this correctly and it will give them the assurance that if they hire you, you won't keep them hanging and having to recruit again in three months' time.

Show that you have put plenty of thought and planning into your career path and that you haven't just chosen to apply for the job in a hurry. Be specific – don't just say that you want to work in advertising but explain why you have applied for that position, with that company. Remember to keep your answer specific to work and how your career journey so far has taken you to this point, to your application with this particular company. Big hint: don't mention your plans to travel, marry or have children, or set up your own business.

Show how your career path developed partly through the influence of successful people in the industry as examples of the careers you would like to emulate. Make a list of some of the world's leading experts in your area and choose who you consider your greatest influences. This will show them that you have done your research and have developed your aspirations partly by learning from role models. It will also give them an understanding of your work ethic and the type of work you want to be doing.

Listen to yourself practise some answers before the interview and find the balance between realistic goals and being overambitious. You don't want to under-sell your abilities or appear to be lacking in drive, but you also don't want to give them the impression that you're after the boss's job. You could say that in five years' time you would like to have learned and progressed enough to be in a position of greater responsibility, perhaps taking on a more managerial or project management role. Make sure you come across as enthusiastic but avoid portraying yourself as a ruthless go-getter who would do anything, including stepping on a lot of toes, to claw your way to the top.

If the distant future appears hazy to you and you honestly have no idea where you will be in five years, then don't feel like you have to lie. However, don't leave it at that – make it clear that you still have ambitions and are excited about the prospect of working for the company. While it's great that your head is focused on the present, you need to convey that you still have a sense of direction and that you're not a lost soul who doesn't have a clue what you want to do until retirement age. Do emphasize that you are very open-minded to whatever opportunities may present themselves and would welcome any training and career development they have to offer. They might see you as the perfect candidate to mould for the future.

## SO WHAT CAN YOU OFFER THAT NO ONE ELSE CAN?

When the interviewer asks you this question, they're getting to the key issue: why should they hire you and not someone else? Recognize this? The wolf in sheep's clothing – 'why do you think you are right for this job' appears here again in yet another guise. Your response to this question should be when you talk about your record of getting things done. Go into specifics from your CV/Resume and portfolio; show an employer your value and what unique qualities you have that would make you a valuable asset to the company. It is here that you could confirm the decision that the interviewer is just about to make – to hire you as the best person for the job. How you sell your unique qualities could clinch the deal and make the difference between a job offer and a rejection letter. This is your chance to really sell yourself and explain how you, with your unique combination of abilities and experience, are the perfect person for the job.

You need to exhibit complete confidence in yourself and what you can bring/offer your potential employer. Tailor your sentences so that you answer clearly and directly, without coming across as being arrogant or pompous. Demonstrate that you are the complete package, complete with the right measure of modesty. While others may have similar skills, show that it is your particular combination of abilities and experiences, plus your great attitude and work ethic that makes you the perfect fit for the job. Keep it succinct and keep it relevant.

So what do you concentrate on in this answer? To risk it becoming too broad, concentrate on your past experiences and achievements, core skills and competencies. Be sure to emphasize your particular strengths or unique experiences that would set you apart from others. Keep in mind what the company is specifically seeking as outlined in the job description, and try to show how you satisfy all the criteria they're looking for. Often, the whole is greater than the sum of its parts, so if your particular skillset or combination of qualities enhances what is required in the job role, you will dazzle them if you just stay calm and answer this question clearly.

It helps invaluably to practise your sales pitch ahead of time so that you can speak confidently and without hesitation. Also show that you have targeted that company specifically and are not just a gun for hire with any company who will offer you a job. Try this sample answer in your own words, describing how it applies to you:

*"I'm the best person for the job. I know there are other candidates who could fill this position, but my passion for excellence sets me apart from the pack. I am committed to always producing the best results. For example..."*

Whatever you do, *don't* criticise the other candidates as a way of promoting your suitability for the job. This will confirm any misgivings that the interview panel have about you.

**Why should we hire you?**

This might seem like a pointless question, each time we get to this stage of the question my first thought is usually "haven't we spent the last forty minutes talking about just that?", just in case you think that way, keep that thought to yourself! This is one of the questions an interviewer usually asks before the end of an interview session. Yes, it's yet another version of "why do you think you're the right person for this job?" Therefore, it is an opportunity for you to sell yourself one last time. Give a list of the great skills and talent you possess that matches with the job description. Don't ramble on with too many details. Just be precise, and you can use hand gestures to jazz up your body language a bit, because you are probably tired at this stage. Summarize your key attributes and you can count each one off on your fingers as you mention it. Make your response clear, simple and short because by this time the interviewers may probably be a little bit tired too and will most likely have dozens more interviews to handle.

**Do you have any questions to ask me?**

*The interview is a two-way process. You are choosing the organisation as much as they are choosing you, so ask questions!* Don't try to ask a question just because you can't really think of any burning issues. Ask questions you really want the answer to. Contrary to advice not to hold up the interviewers with a question at this stage, asking no questions suggests a lack of interest! Research the company carefully and you will find questions naturally arising. Don't ask more than four to five questions unless you are getting encouragement, as other interviewees may be waiting. Focus on questions that show your interest in the work itself rather than the rewards it will bring. Ask about training and career progression in preference to pay, pensions, holidays and parking!

Prepare questions in advance; note them down on a card to bring with you. If all your prepared questions have been answered during the interview just say what you had planned to ask, and that you have already covered the answers. You can also mention here anything that has not been covered but that is important to your application. It often happens that during the interview all the points that you had noted down to ask about will be covered before you get to this stage. In this situation, you can respond as follows: Interviewer: *"Well, that seems to have covered everything: is there anything you would like to ask me?"*

Interviewee: *"Thank you: I'd made a note to ask about your appraisal system and the study arrangements for professional exams, but we went over those earlier and I really feel you've covered everything that I need to know at this moment."*

You can also use this opportunity to tell the interviewer anything about yourself that they have not raised during the interview but which you feel is important to your application. Don't feel you have to wait until this point to ask questions - if the chance to ask a question seems to arise naturally in the course of the interview, take it! Remember that a traditional interview is a two-way conversation - with a purpose. It is true that one of the unspoken rules of interviews is that the interviewers are in control and you must follow their lead. Break this fundamental rule at your peril. But this doesn't mean you have to sit there with your tongue glued to the roof of your mouth if you really need to ask something valid during the interview. It's better to leave knowing the answer, and leaving the interviewer assured that you can follow direction or procedure while also being assertive enough to find out what you need to know.

No matter how strange an interviewer's question seems to be, try to answer it. Even if the interview panel asks you to talk about your childhood or tell them a joke, you must attempt to do your best. If you're anything like me, you could have a fantastic sense of humour but suffer with memory-freeze as soon as you are asked to tell a joke. Have a few up your sleeve because this question could very easily be tested, to see if you're likely to have a sense of humour with your colleagues. Unless the interviewer's question is illegal, don't ever say *"that's an odd question"* or ask *"why do you want to know that?"* If they do, and they are putting you on the spot, decide how to answer it based on the context that you find yourself in.

**What about discussing money?**

This always feels like a dirty subject in the interview, but the reality is that most of us work because we need to earn a living. Enjoying your job is of course hugely important – it makes all the difference between being happy and being stressed and gloomy throughout your working life. The truth is that a lot of people wouldn't work if they could afford not to. This is not to say that they wouldn't find plenty to do that makes for a busy day. Most of us, given the choice, would work on all the things we are passionate about if we didn't need to work in paid employment. Music lovers could learn an instrument … would-be gymnasts could hit the training bars … sailing enthusiasts could learn how to spend months out at sea … (insert your own dreams here and take comfort from them).

Interviewers often see candidates asking about the pay and benefits too soon in the interview process as being rather tactless. If you need to pass through several rounds of interviews, only talk about money in the final round. The best time to talk about money is after you've been offered the job – most jobs have a confirmation period that gives you seven to ten days to make your mind up. Failing that scenario, only talk about money if the interviewers ask you about it first. The exception to this is if you are going for a sales or marketing job, where it's entirely appropriate to ask what commissions you are entitled to.

Bear in mind too that many interview candidates now ask about the benefits of working for the company, in addition to their salary. For example, free healthcare, expenses, company car, laptop, gym membership, number of days holiday per year, and so on. If these are something you want to find out more about in addition to your salary, don't be afraid to ask.

**Finish the interview by thanking them for their time!**

So having digested everything in this book you should be more than prepared to storm every job you apply for, from writing your CV/ Resume to preparing for and attending an interview. We'll wrap up in the conclusion with a checklist, and just so we don't conclude this book on a serious note, I've added a zany look at "what not to do in an interview".

# Conclusion:

# CARDINAL RULES, CARDINAL SINS AND HOW NOT TO DO AN INTERVIEW

Here's an "at a glance" checklist of what to do before and during the interview

- Start your research at least a week before. Much of it will be generic and will be helpful for attending other interviews too.
- Eat well the day before and have a good night sleep. Eat breakfast on the day of the interview – being nervous can cause your blood sugar levels to drop too low, leaving you feeling weak and shaky.
- Dress smartly and subtly. Trouser-suits (trouser-suits or skirt-suits for women), with a plain, crisp well-ironed shirt. Make sure that everything you are wearing fits you properly so that you're not uncomfortable in the interview.
- Make a friendly, confident entrance – smile, shake hands firmly and warmly, don't sit until you are invited to do so.
- Tea or coffee? Only if your hands are not shaking and you feel that it might help calm you. Just remember that both contain caffeine and are likely to make your anxiety worse.
- Be articulate – we all use "er, you know, like, whatever, do you get me?" etc. in our normal speech but try to rehearse speaking slowly, professionally and clearly.

- Take a moment to think about the answer to a question if you are not sure of how you will respond. "Excuse me, I just need a moment to think about this" is fine to use.

- Be pleasant and relaxed – don't bare your teeth through a fake smile at the interview panel because you are so anxious! Smile, be warm and affable, and you will be surprised at how adopting this attitude really does help you to relax.

- Show that you have researched the company and explain some aspects that you like about it – their values, staff care attitudes, etc.

- Ask questions about the company when you are giving an answer – it shows that you are already thinking about how you will fit the role, and how the role fits with the company's practice.

- Use stories to illustrate examples – they lighten the atmosphere and show very clearly what you are trying to explain. (Use in moderation though!)

- Remember that the interviewers will feel anxious and under pressure too, to find the best recruit.

- Strengths and weaknesses – they are not trying to catch you out by asking you about your weaknesses, they want to see that you have been able to turn a negative situation into a positive one.

- Think of all the worst attributes of a colleague: arrogant, terrible team player, bad-tempered, lazy, argumentative and mean. When you prepare your questions make sure to illustrate through what you say that you are the opposite to all of these.

- Don't complain about your previous jobs or bosses. Rather than being negative, professionally frame your reasons for leaving previous jobs or disputes with previous employers. Example: "Our managing director explained to me that my boss was having some personal problems, which were affecting his work relationships. Once I knew this I was able to deal with his negativity knowing that it wasn't really about me or about my standard of work"

- Be prepared to explain gaps in your CV/Resume. For younger people you might have been travelling or taking time out to do something else you love. For older applicants, employers do expect to see that you have real and valid reasons for gaps in your employment. These are easier to explain if you negotiated a career break with your employer at that time.
- If questions come to mind during the interview, write them down so that you have them ready to ask later.
- Close the interview by asking what you need to. If you have nothing to ask, ask the interviewers to talk about the positive experiences they have had with this company. You could also ask them about how their career path led to this position.
- **Close the interview by thanking them for their time and say that you have enjoyed finding out more about the company.**

## TEN CARDINAL SINS OF INTERVIEWING

One of the most common pieces of advice I have given in this book is to have answers as well prepared as possible in advance of the interview. On the other hand, be prepared for some unfortunate unforeseen circumstances. Things don't always go according to plan. Your little baby might be sick on your interview jacket two minutes before you put it on to run out the door. In the interview itself, many candidates get it wrong sometimes by making some cardinal mistakes listed below. Any of these can turn a potentially good day into a sore one:

### Turning up late

This is the worst thing that can ever happen to you at an interview. I would rather you turn up late for your own wedding than for an interview; it's a huge NO-NO!!! The interviewers may have a packed schedule of interviews for the day, and a late arrival almost certainly makes them feel annoyed with you before you've even met. It also shows a lack of interest or commitment to wanting to make a good impression by getting there on time.

I once turned up late for an interview, this was because I didn't plan ahead neither did I give ample time for unforeseen circumstances like train delays, road works, traffics etc. unknown to me, there were train works going on that day, which delayed my journey for a good 40 minutes, obviously I dint get the job. The truth is interviewers don't care about all these; all they want is for you to be there well and on time.

Always carefully plan your journey to the interview. Make sure that you know the route to take whether you are driving or travelling by public transport. And plan in plenty of time for contingencies. Running into a road traffic accident on the motorway could hold you up for an hour. The clutch could go in your car. Try to have someone on standby to pick you up and drive you there if something disastrous goes wrong. It's better to be there early find a nearby café/restaurant to while away the time. You can have a drink and one final run through your questions. Take a paper with you and catch up on what's happening in the world in case the interviewers want to make chitchat about the news or current affairs.

Remember that every company is affected by PEST:

- **Politics**
- **Economics**
- **Sociology**
- **Technology**

In other words, what is going on in domestic or international politics, world finance, the social mood of the time, and advances in IT and machinery, has a direct effect on whether businesses grow or go under.

If you are running late for any reason, call ahead with your apologies to give the interviewers as much advance warning as possible.

## Getting the dress code wrong

Showing up for an interview and realizing that you're dressed inappropriately will make you feel incredibly foolish and will drain you of your confidence. Even if the organisation has a casual dress code, it is vital that you dress smartly and formally for an interview. If you are in any doubt, you can always call HR to ask about the dress code. Don't allow yourself to be fobbed off by a receptionist who probably won't know what the interviewers may be wearing for the interview. Speak to one of the interviewers if you can, and check with them. Alternatively you can ask one of their personal assistants, or check the staff pages on their website to see how highly they place their dress code.

### Being rude to receptionists

Most candidates ruin their chances by being a bit off-hand with a receptionist, secretary or a personal assistant. You need to be very careful because when you walk into a company premises for the first time you don't know who is who; s/he can be a manager or a supervisor standing in for a receptionist for that day or for a few hours. In any case, the position of the person should never dictate whether you are polite to them or not. Everyone deserves to be treated with respect, and make sure to demonstrate this by being affable with everyone.

Interviewers often ask receptionists or their PA's what they thought of you, and the wrong words or the wrong gesture at someone can be fatal. Rudeness is one of the main things that is taken into account by the interviewers. If they hire you, you will represent their company. If you are likely to come across as being nasty to people, you will be exited through their back door. You are being observed and evaluated from the moment you arrive at an employer's premises. Every single person working within the organisation who interacts with you or who even sees you can potentially feed information back to the interviewers.

### Getting off to a shaky start

As hard as it is to maintain your cool at the beginning of an interview, you must remember this: first impressions count! If you appear nervous in your first few minutes you make it much harder for yourself as you'll spend the rest of the interview internally beating yourself up for getting off to the wrong start. You'll have to work hard to change the interviewers' initial impression of you. Follow these tips for making your first couple of minutes go smoothly:

- Smile broadly (but not sheepishly) as you enter the room
- Say hello and something like "It's good to meet you" or "Great to meet you". Say it with enthusiasm.
- Maintain eye contact while saying hello.
- Give the interviewers a firm (but not vice-like) hand-shake then follow their lead by sitting down only when you are asked to.
- Create the impression that you're an upbeat and optimistic person. Compliment the interviewers about their organisation or make a positive comment about anything that strikes you:
- "I'm terribly impressed by this building – I really like your reception area."
- "It's great to be here. And, by the way, your receptionists are so friendly."
- "This is such a good location for your offices – how long have you been based here?"
- Make your comment genuine and say it sincerely! It also gives you a bit of breathing space before the interview gets under way.

**Giving a monologue**

Interviewers don't have time for lengthy, repetitive interviews – they may have shortlisted 50 candidates for certain jobs – that's over 300 hours of interviewing. So make your answers interesting, engaging and precise. Don't bore the interviewers by speaking too long and making them feel under pressure to make up lost time. Interviewers have a short attention span because they are trying to take in a lot of detail all at once. But, unfortunately, they are also often inept at interrupting candidates, even when those candidates may be boring them to death. Interviewers are human – they may often just sit there mutely, pretending to appear interested while secretly thinking about what they may have for dinner that evening.

Try to speak for no more than two minutes at a time. Even when the interviewers seem rapt, check with them halfway through a lengthy answer by asking: "Is this useful? Shall I go on?" Interviewers are generally polite enough to maintain eye contact even if they are incredibly bored. But they often fail to nod when they're not interested.

Get Your Dream Job

So watch out for this tell-tale sign and either speak briefly or inject a bit more energy into your performance if no one's nodding.

**Answering in monosyllables**

Nerves can get the better of some candidates and cause them to dry up and become speechless under the stress of being interviewed. Failing to give enough detail is another fatal mistake, because your answers just float with no context to ground them. Do your absolute best to avoid answering in monosyllables. Remember that even if the interviewers ask you a closed question, such as "Did you have a good journey?" you should answer in a sentence or two.

This means not answering with just a "yes" or "no", which makes the interviewers feel as if speaking to you is like trying to get blood out of a stone. Smalltalk and chitchat are all ways of assessing you – if you have a corporate lunch with a client you are bound to feel under pressure too, but you need to be comfortable to provide open answers to these little icebreakers. An open response to "did you have a good journey?" would be: "Yes, thanks, my journey was great although there was a lot of traffic on the road" or "my journey was pretty smooth. Thanks for asking."

Speak for a couple of sentences for every question that you're asked. For most questions – especially those asking you for examples of situations that you've been in, aim to speak for at least five or six sentences. You can practise timing these at home with a clock to give you an idea of how you can answer a question elaborately, but not tediously either.

# FAILING THE STUCK IN THE LIFT TEST

Imagine this scenario: You're stuck in a lift with the interviewer. The lift breaks down and you are waiting to be rescued, or you are both are going to the 20th floor. Would you be able to have an interesting conversation with the interviewer or would you be there praying to get off the lift. From the interviewer's point of view, being put in this situation with two equally skilled and experienced candidates, the

137

interviewers are going to plump for the one who is more interesting, easy going and clearly shows their individuality. So put simply, the stuck in the lift test is an assessment of whether the interviewers like you and want to work with you.

My advice is this: try to showcase yourself as an interesting, fun to be with candidate. The interviewers have had yet another long, wearying day; your presence should cheer them up. Don't be just another candidate being interviewed. Try to be different and leave them with a good memory of you; you might just be the first person they will be calling back. Think of choosing a house – on the brochure you see eight, maybe nine that look perfect. You visit the first two, they're lovely, you like them. By the time you are visiting the sixth, you've completely forgotten about the first two. The one you remember is the one that makes you feel that it has got that "extra something" that is not just a 100% match with your requirements. It has individuality to it too that leaves it stuck in your memory long after you have viewed it.

## INTERVIEWS: HOW NOT TO DO IT ...

- A candidate had a fizzy drink just before his interview and spent the whole interview burping
- The nightmare you have the night before: an interviewee comes dressed in pyjamas and slippers
- A female interviewee wore a personal stereo and said she could listen to me and the music at the same time
- When I asked him about his hobbies, he stood up and started tap dancing around the office
- A candidate pulled out a camera and took a photo. He said he collected photos of everyone who interviewed him
- Without saying a word, the candidate stood up and walked out during the middle of the interview
- A candidate still drunk after a night out with his friends handcuffed himself to the interview desk and claimed he was making a political protest against The Establishment

- With more than a touch of arrogance, a candidate said he was so well-qualified that if he didn't get the job, it would prove that the company's management was incompetent
- I asked a female candidate about the many jobs she had had and she said "I get bored easily"
- Another one brought his mother to the interview and let her answer the questions.
- Enthusiastic about showing off her passions and interests, a female candidate sang her answers to the questions
- Someone dozed off during the interview
- A male candidate dunked his biscuit in his tea and lost it – he became preoccupied with fishing it out and lost focus completely.
- A chaotic female announced that she hadn't had lunch and proceeded to eat during the interview
- An easy-go-lucky male said he would demonstrate loyalty by having the company logo tattooed on his arm
- A female candidate said that she would prefer a job offer from one of the company's competitors
- A male fantasist said he never finished high school because he was kidnapped and kept in a wardrobe · Interviewer: What is your date of birth? Interviewee: May the 15th Interviewer: Which year?
  Interviewee: Every year
- Interviewer: Tell me a word that has more than 10 letters in it? Interviewee: Post-box

… So however badly you think you've messed up at interviews before, it can't have been as bad as the examples above! My hope for this book is that you can use it as a guide and a strategy plan for preparing your job application. Once those interviews start to roll out to you, hopefully you will be shortlisted to attend the right one, and land yourself the perfect job. Happy job hunting and good luck!

**NOW GO GET THAT JOB……..**

*Ebere Ujam-Ojadua*

**References** *Dreamstime.com*
*http://www.careerfaqs.com.au/careers/interviewquestions-and-tips/how-to-answer-interview-questions/*
*http://www.kent.ac.uk/careers/CV/Resume/CV/ResumeProf iles.htm*

Printed in the United States
By Bookmasters